SACRIFICE

AGE OF BRONZE
Volume 2

SACRIFICE

by Eric Shanower

image

Age of Bronze
Volume 2
Sacrifice
Copyright © 2004 by Eric Shanower. All rights reserved.

ISBN 1-58240-360-0 (hardcover)
ISBN 1-58240-399-6 (softcover)

Published by Image Comics, Inc.
Office of Publication: 1071 N. Batavia Street, Suite A
Orange, CA 92867
Image and its logos are ® and © 2004 by Image Comics, Inc. All rights reserved.

Erik Larsen *Publisher*
Todd McFarlane *President*
Marc Silvestri *CEO*
Jim Valentino *Vice-President*

Eric Stephenson *Managing Editor*
Brett Evans *Production Manager*
Allen Hui *Web Developer*
Tim Hegarty *Booktrade/International Rights*
Traci Hale *Controller*
Cindie Espinoza *Accounting Assistant*
Jon Malin *Production Assistant*

The story of *Sacrifice* was originally serialized in the comic book series
Age of Bronze, issues 10 though 19.

First printing September 2004

Visit the *Age of Bronze* website at
www.age-of-bronze.com

Age of Bronze is a trademark of Eric Shanower.

Printed in Canada.

Friends of Troy is an organization for those interested in Troy and its legends.
It supports the ongoing activities of the International Troy Excavation Project.
All Friends of Troy receive the annual newsletter and updates on Troy-related news.
Friends are welcome at Troy and are given guided tours of the site and excavation.
If you would like to become a Friend of Troy, send your name and address to

Institute for Mediterranean Studies
7086 Aracoma Drive
Cincinnati, OH 45237
USA

Phone: 513/631-8049
Fax: 513/631-1715
E-mail: studies@usa.net
Website: www.studies.org
Or see: www.uni-tuebingen.de/troia/eng/freunde.html

For information on the TROIA – FOUNDATION which supports
the International Troy Excavation Project, see the website
www.uni-tuebingen.de/troia/eng/troiastiftung.html

For Dad,
whose ships don't go astray.

"I was cut off from hope in that sad place
  Which men call'd Aulis in those iron years:
My father held his hand upon his face;
  I, blinded with my tears,

"Still strove to speak: my voice was thick with sighs
  As in a dream. Dimly I could descry
The stern black-bearded kings with wolfish eyes,
  Waiting to see me die.

"The high masts flicker'd as they lay afloat;
  The crowds, the temples, waver'd, and the shore;
The bright death quiver'd at the victim's throat—
  Touch'd—and I knew no more."

—Alfred Lord Tennyson
"A Dream of Fair Women," 1833-53
lines 105-116

Contents

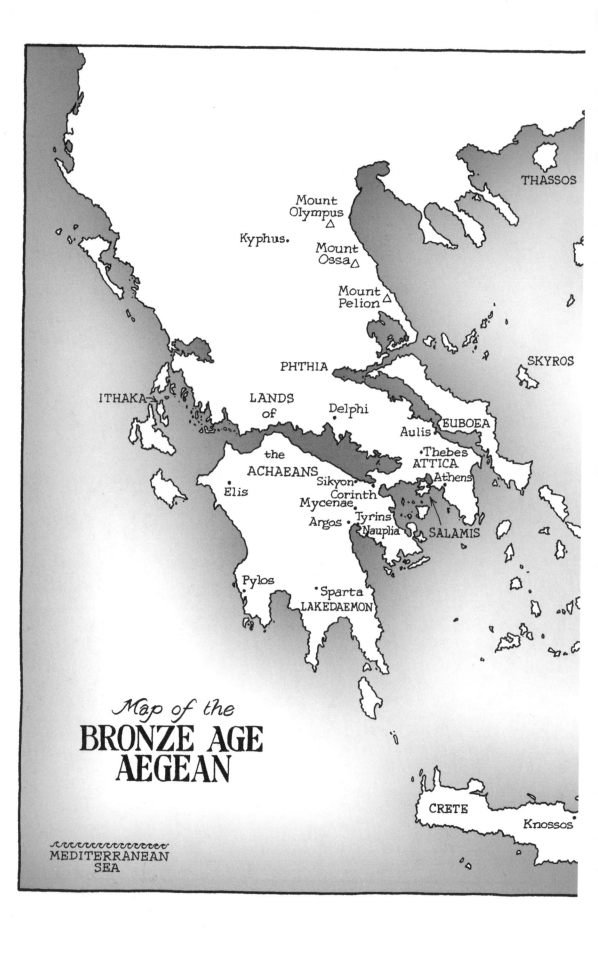

THASSOS

Mount
Olympus
△

Kyphus.

Mount
Ossa △

Mount
Pelion △

SKYROS

PHTHIA

ITHAKA

LANDS
of

Delphi

EUBOEA

Aulis

the
ACHAEANS

•Thebes
ATTICA

Sikyon•
Corinth
Mycenae•

•Athens

Elis•

Argos• •Tyrins
Nauplia

SALAMIS

Pylos•

•Sparta
LAKEDAEMON

Map of the
BRONZE AGE
AEGEAN

CRETE

Knossos •

MEDITERRANEAN
SEA

BLACK SEA

THRACE

SAMOTHRACE
IMBROS

TENEDOS
LEMNOS
Dardania

○Troy

Mount
△ Ida

Thebes

MYSIA

LESBOS

ARZAWA

CHIOS

AEGEAN
SEA

SAMOS

Miletos

DELOS

LYCIA

Halikarnassos

THERA

Knidos

RHODES

to →
KOLCHIS

Troy

HATTI

Hattusas

Karchemish

AMURRU
to →
ASSYRIA
Kadesh
to
BABYLON
→

CRETE

CYPRUS

Sidon

EGYPT

Memphis

Miles
Kilometers

0 10   50   100   200
0   50   100   200   300

OUR STORY SO FAR

During the Late Bronze Age—about the 13th century BCE—the powerful city of Troy flourishes under the Great King Priam's rule. Years before, Priam's sister Hesione was captured by Achaean raiders during an assault on Troy. Now Priam commands Paris, a prince of Troy recently reunited with his father and his mother Hekuba, to bring Hesione back. Priam's daughter Kassandra and her twin brother Helenus predict calamity, but no one takes their warnings seriously.

Accompanied by his cousin Aeneas, Paris sails to the Achaean city of Sparta where Menelaus is king. Paris forgets his pregnant lover, the mountain nymph Oenone, and ignoring his brother Hektor's warning to follow their father Priam's instructions, he seduces Menelaus's wife Helen away from Sparta with her serving women and infant son Pleisthenes. They sail to Cyprus, then to Sidon.

Helen's brothers Kastor and Polydeukes pursue, but are lost in a storm at sea.

Menelaus is eager to recover his wife, while his brother Agamemnon, king of Mycenae and High King of the Achaeans, is eager to gain Troy's control of rich trade routes through the Hellespont. So they summon the many Achaean kings who once swore an oath to help Helen's husband for her sake. At the bay at Aulis a massive army with hundreds of ships and thousands of men assembles. The army pledges to follow High King Agamemnon as commander in an attack on Troy.

The Achaean priestess Thetis foresees the death of her son Achilles at Troy. To circumvent this, she takes the boy from his teacher, the kentaur Cheiron, and hides him, disguised as a girl called Pyrrha, among the daughters of Lykomedes on the island of Skyros. There, Achilles rapes Lykomedes's eldest daughter Deidamia, who bears a son. Deidamia calls the child Pyrrhus; Achilles calls him Neoptolemus.

A prophecy foretells that if Odysseus, king of Ithaka, goes to Troy with the army, he'll return home to his wife Penelope and son Telemachus after twenty years, alone and unrecognized. To avoid this fate, Odysseus pretends to be mad. But Palamedes, prince of Nauplia, exposes Odysseus's ploy, thus earning his enmity.

Kalchas, Trojan priest of the sun god, has visions that show him Troy's fall. He joins the Achaeans, leaving his recently widowed daughter Cressida at Troy in the care of her uncle Pandarus. The Trojan prince Troilus falls in love with Cressida, but Pandarus discourages Troilus from pursuing her prematurely.

All signs point to eventual success for the Achaean army. The Delphic oracle predicts Achaean victory over Troy, contingent, however, upon conflict among Achaeans. And Kalchas foretells Achaean triumph in the tenth year, provided that Achilles joins the army.

Odysseus tricks Achilles into shedding his disguise and brings him to Aulis. Achilles assumes leadership of his father Peleus's Myrmidons from Phthia, choosing a short life fighting gloriously at Troy rather than a long life in obscurity.

After Palamedes remedies a food shortage by bringing supplies from Delos, the army at last sets sail for war with Troy.

SACRIFICE

ANOTHER FINE FLEECE TO ADD TO TROY'S RICHES!

BY ORDER OF PRIAM, ALL ABLE-BODIED MEN, TO ARMS!

WHAT IS IT?

WHAT'S GOING ON?

KEBRIONES! POLYDAMAS! WHAT IS ALL THIS?

HEKTOR!

A LARGE FLEET OF SHIPS IS MAKING FOR THE SOUTH BAY--THEY DON'T LOOK LIKE MERCHANTS.

RAIDERS?

MOST LIKELY. PRIAM'S COMMANDED US TO REINFORCE THE GARRISON AT THE BAY.

HAH! SHEARING KNIVES AGAINST PIRATES!

ALL WE REALLY NEED IS A SHOW OF FORCE.

TROY'S MIGHT IS KNOWN THROUGHOUT THE WORLD. THEY'D BE FOOLS TO TRY TO FIGHT US.

DRAW HER UP THE BEACH! **WELL UP!**

HELLO! HELLO, EVERYONE--

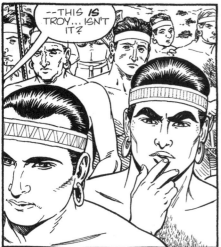

--THIS **IS** TROY... ISN'T IT?

THAT'S RIGHT. THE MIGHTY CITY OF TROY LIES NEARBY IN THE PLAIN OF IDA. ITS GREAT KING PRIAM COMMANDS ME TO ASSESS A PORTION OF CARGO FROM EVERY SHIP THAT BEACHES HERE.

I HAVEN'T FORGOTTEN. BUT IT SEEMS THE TROJANS HAVE FORGOTTEN **ME**--

PARIS!

PARIS, **PRINCE OF TROY!** AND MY SHIPS ARE FILLED WITH **RICHES** FOR PRIAM-- TREASURES FROM SIDON AND EGYPT!

COME! I NEED MEN TO HELP CARRY IT ALL INTO **TROY!**

BUT DO YOU BRING A WOMAN FROM ACHAEA? **THAT'S** WHAT WILL INTEREST PRIAM.

AENEAS-- COUSIN!

IT'S BEEN TOO LONG, HEKTOR, *MUCH* TOO LONG. I WASN'T SURE I'D EVER SEE THE PLAIN OF IDA AGAIN.

HAVE YOU SENT ANYONE TO TELL PRIAM THAT WE'VE ARRIVED?

NO, NOT YET.

THEN LEND ME A CHARIOT AND *I'LL* GO!

RIGHT! KEBRIONES, DID YOU HEAR THAT?

WHAT'S HAPPENING NOW, AITHRA?

AENEAS IS RIDING OFF IN A CHARIOT--TO ANNOUNCE TO THE CITY OUR ARRIVAL, NO DOUBT.

CHECK MY BACK HAIR AGAIN, KLYMENE. AND IS MY MAKE-UP RIGHT? THIS LIGHT IS TOO DIM!

GENTLY, CHILD. YOU LOOK AS LOVELY AS EVER. STOP FUSSING.

OH, AITHRA ...IT'S JUST --THIS IS SO IMPORTANT,,, AND I'VE WAITED SO LONG.

WE'VE SPENT SO LONG SKIMMING THE SEA FROM ONE KING'S GUEST CHAMBER TO THE NEXT. HERE...THERE ...NEVER ANYWHERE FOR VERY LONG--NEVER BELONGING.

NOW WE'VE REACHED TROY-- TROY AT *LAST!* WHERE HE BELONGS. AND NOW THAT I'M HIS, WHERE *I* BELONG, TOO. HOW I'VE *LONGED* FOR THIS DAY.

WE CERTAINLY *HAVE* TAKEN OUR TIME ABOUT GETTING HERE.

NOW I'LL MEET THEM-- PRIAM, HEKUBA--ALL THE REST. WHAT IF I CAN'T WIN THEM OVER, AITHRA? WHAT IF--

NOW, NOW, YOU DON'T NEED TO WORRY -- YOU'RE HELEN. *HELEN!* BLESSED BY THE GODDESS. JUST BE YOURSELF, BE *HELEN*. AND NO MATTER WHAT THEY MIGHT TELL THEM- SELVES THEY *OUGHT* TO THINK, THEY'LL DO NOTHING BUT LOVE YOU.

THAT'S WHAT ALWAYS HAPPENS, ISN'T IT?

IS IT? I GUESS IT IS... BUT--

COME, IT'S TIME TO START MAKING THEM ALL LOVE YOU.

YES.

PARIS, HERE'S YOUR HELEN--

--HELEN OF TROY!

GREAT KING, THE WATCH REPORTS A CHARIOT FROM THE SOUTH BAY ENTERING THE SKAEAN GATE.

GOOD. WE'LL SOON KNOW WHAT THIS UNFAMILIAR FLEET BRINGS--

GREAT KING! GREAT KING, PARDON ME--

I WILL, CRESSIDA...

...SINCE YOU HAVE REFRAINED FROM INVADING MY HALL FOR SOME MONTHS. BUT HERE YOU ARE AGAIN--

GREAT KING, EVERYONE IS SAYING A HUGE FLEET HAS LANDED--DOZENS AND DOZENS OF SHIPS! DO THEY...DO THEY BRING ANY NEWS OF MY *FATHER*?

GO HOME AND WAIT QUIETLY, CRESSIDA. WE'RE STILL WAITING TO LEARN WHO THE NEWCOMERS ARE. IF THEY KNOW ANYTHING ABOUT KALCHAS, I'LL SEND A SERVANT TO TELL YOU IMMEDIATELY.

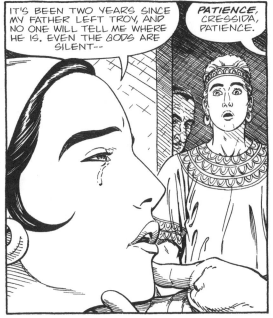

IT'S BEEN TWO YEARS SINCE MY FATHER LEFT TROY, AND NO ONE WILL TELL ME WHERE HE IS. EVEN THE GODS ARE SILENT--

PATIENCE, CRESSIDA, PATIENCE.

YOUR FATHER GIVES *EXCELLENT* ADVICE, TROILUS.

PANDARUS! HER AGONY'S LASTED FAR TOO LONG-- *SOMEONE* HAS TO HELP HER.

IT'S NOT AS BAD AS YOU THINK. MY DAUGHTERS AND I HAVE MANAGED TO MAKE HER HAPPY IN OUR HOME.

I KNOW, I KNOW--IT'S NOTHING LIKE THE HAPPINESS A CERTAIN TROJAN PRINCE COULD GIVE HER, HOLDING HER IN HIS VIGOROUS ARMS. BUT IN HER EYES YOU'RE STILL A BOY. SHE ISN'T READY FOR YOUR COMFORT--*YET*.

WHEN?

AS PRIAM SAYS, TROILUS-- *PATIENCE*...

GREAT KING--AENEAS, PRINCE OF DARDANIA, HAS ARRIVED FROM THE SOUTH BAY AND ENTERS YOUR HALL!

AENEAS?

SALUTATIONS, GREAT KING! WE'VE FINALLY RETURNED TO TROY.

PARIS ACCOMPANIES YOU?

I PLEDGED TO BRING PARIS BACK TO TROY. THAT'S WHAT I'VE DONE.

THAT'S SO, GREAT KING. PARIS AND --AND THOSE WITH HIM--ARE APPROACHING THE CITY NOW.

I'VE HEARD REPORTS-- *RUMORS*-- THAT HESIONE HASN'T RE- TURNED WITH YOU-- THAT *ANOTHER* WOMAN...

PARIS MUST EXPLAIN THE WOMAN HE BRINGS FROM ACHAEA. MY RESPONSI- BILITY WAS TO BRING YOUR SON BACK TO YOU. THAT'S FULFILLED.

AND IN THAT REGARD, I WISH TO CLAIM MY REWARD -- YOUR DAUGHTER KREUSA--

NOT NOW, WE'LL DISCUSS THAT LATER. THIS WOMAN MUST NOT ENTER THE CITY.

IDAEUS, SEND WORD TO HAVE THEM STOPPED AT THE GATE! AND GET MY CHARIOT READY!

AT ONCE, GREAT KING.

GREAT KING, I'LL FOLLOW YOU.

SO WILL I!

ME, TOO!

IT'S **YOURS**, MY LOVE-- THE GREATEST CITY IN THE WORLD.

WE'RE **HERE**-- IT'S **TRUE**! TROY.

I WANT TO FEEL ITS WARM STONES BENEATH MY OWN HANDS...

HA HA! IN A FEW MOMENTS YOU CAN TOUCH ANY PART OF IT YOU WANT--

--JUST LIKE YOU CAN TOUCH ANY PART OF **ME**!

PARIS!

GREAT KING! FATHER!

I CAME TO SEE WHETHER THE NEWS OF YOUR RETURN COULD REALLY BE TRUE--YOU'VE BEEN AWAY SO LONG.

IT LOOKS LIKE EVERYONE ELSE HAD THE SAME IDEA.

LOOK, HELEN! THE WHOLE CITY'S COME TO WELCOME US!

WHAT DO THEIR MURMURS MEAN? ARE THEY WELCOMING ME? OR JUDGING ME?

SO *THAT'S* WHAT AN ACHAEAN WOMAN LOOKS LIKE!

IF THEY'RE ALL LIKE HER, LET'S BRING OVER SOME *MORE!*

NO WOMAN'S WORTH STARTING A *WAR* OVER.

SHE'D KEEP A MAN WARM AT NIGHT, THOUGH.

LOOK AT HER HAIR SHINE IN THE SUNLIGHT!

EASY TO LOOK AT ON THE OUTSIDE, BUT HARD AS BRONZE INSIDE. I KNOW THE TYPE.

PARIS, WHERE IS THE WOMAN I SENT YOU TO ACHAEA FOR, MY SISTER HESIONE, WHOM I'VE LONG AWAITED?

GREAT KING, I'VE RETURNED WITH A WOMAN WHO IS ALL HESIONE IS AND MORE! HELEN, DAUGHTER OF TYNDAREUS OF LAKEDAE--

I *KNOW* WHO SHE IS.

WHERE IS *HESIONE*?

WAIT, GREAT KING! LOOK AT THE TREASURES I'VE BROUGHT YOU--NOT ONLY FROM ACHAEA, BUT FROM FAR AND WIDE!

IVORY FROM CYPRUS-- GOLD FROM PHOENICIA --PERFUME FROM EGYPT--

KING PHALIS OF SIDON FELL BY MY HAND WHEN WE SACKED HIS CITY.

DO YOU MEAN *YOU* ARE THE RAIDER WHO STORMED SIDON LAST YEAR?

YES! NOW SIDON'S RICHES FILL SHIP AFTER SHIP--ALL FOR *YOU*, GREAT KING!

EXCEPT FOR THE *WOMAN*. HE'S KEEPING HER FOR *HIMSELF*!

IF IT'S WOMEN YOU WANT, HERE THEY ARE! *HIGH-BORN* WOMEN. LOOK, THIS IS THE SISTER OF THE GREAT ACHAEAN HERO PEIRITHOUS. AND THESE DAUGHTERS OF SPARTAN NOBLES WILL MAKE EXCELLENT WIVES FOR MY BROTHERS!

I'LL TAKE THE ONE IN THE CHARIOT.

I--NO... NO...

DON'T WANT ONE, HELENUS? THEN I'LL TAKE THE REST OF THEM.

THAT CATTLEHERDER SACKED SIDON? IMPOSSIBLE!

MAYBE NOT. THOSE CLOAKS SAY HE DID IT. EXCELLENT QUALITY.

WHO WOULDN'T SACK CITIES TO IMPRESS A WOMAN LIKE THAT!

SHE'S BEAUTIFUL, ISN'T SHE, LAODIKE?

YES. I WONDER WHAT SHE'S LIKE...

DID YOU REALLY SACK SIDON?

BY THE GODS, KREUSA, YOU WOULDN'T BELIEVE THE FOOLHARDY STUNTS PARIS MANEUVERED US INTO!

I'M AMAZED THEY MADE IT BACK TO TROY AT ALL!

BUT TO PERISH FOR LOVE WOULD BE SO ROMANTIC!

QUIET, I CAN'T HEAR PRIAM!

...FAILED TO ACCOMPLISH THE TASK I SET YOU.

BUT...

...AT LEAST YOU MANAGED TO BRING AN ACHAEAN PRINCESS WE CAN TRADE FOR HESIONE.

WHAT? I DIDN'T BRING HER HERE TO TRADE!

PARIS, A MAN WHO CARRIES OFF A KING'S WIFE IS CERTAINLY *BRAVE*, BUT NOT VERY SMART. PRIAM KNOWS BEST. DO AS HE SAYS.

NO! HELEN IS MY *WIFE!*

SHE IS NOT YOUR WIFE UNLESS *I* SAY SO!

WAIT.

PRIAM OF TROY, GREAT KING...

THEN I HAVE NOTHING LEFT...

...ONLY... PUH--

...PARIS?

...THE CHILDREN...

CHILDREN?

YES, GREAT KING. THIS IS MY CHILD, PARIS'S SON, AGANUS.

MY GRANDSON.

HE MUST REMAIN IN TROY WHEN YOU LEAVE.

DON'T TURN REPROACHFUL EYES TOWARD ME, QUEEN OF SPARTA. YOU'VE LEFT A CHILD BEHIND ALREADY. ANOTHER SHOULD MAKE NO DIFFERENCE. BUT YOU SAID *CHILDREN* --THAT OTHER?

PLEISTHENES IS MY SON BY MENELAUS. I--I HAVE NO MORE CHILDREN BY PARIS.

WAIT! THERE'S ONE MORE--

...GROWING IN HER WOMB! SHE CARRIES THE TROJAN ROYAL LINE WITHIN HER RIGHT NOW!

THE GODS PLAY US FOR FOOLS.

DAUGHTER...

IT'S TRUE, PRIAM. WHAT CHOICE IS LEFT?

TROJANS, MY SON PARIS RETURNS WITH A NEW WIFE. THEY MUST PLEDGE THEIR UNITY IN THE TEMPLES, THEN FOR EIGHT DAYS THE WHOLE CITY WILL CELEBRATE THE MARRIAGE FEAST! JOIN ME IN WELCOMING HELEN TO TROY!

LISTEN TO THEM CHEER!

WELCOME TO TROY, SISTER.

AT LAST, AT LAST!

I CAN'T BELIEVE THAT COW-TURD PARIS IS GETTING AWAY WITH THIS.

HELENUS, WHAT'S WRONG?

UH... JUST A HEADACHE.

I WONDER HOW LONG UNTIL THE WIND CARRIES ACHAEAN WARSHIPS TO US.

THEY'LL NEVER ATTACK US -- WE'D SLAUGHTER THEM!

GREAT KING, I PRAY THAT TROY WON'T COME TO REGRET THIS DAY.

THE GODS HAVE DECIDED, ANTENOR. TROY'S FATE RESTS IN THEIR HANDS.

BUT WHATEVER HAPPENS, I HAVE TO ADMIT I LIKE HER. YOU SAW THE WAY SHE STOOD UP TO ME...

FIRST,
THE TEMPLE
OF THE SUN GOD...

PARIS, COME
PLEDGE YOUR
UNION.

NOW, IF ALL THE ATTENDANTS
DIDN'T RUN OFF TO THE
SKAEAN GATE WITH
EVERYONE ELSE...

AH, GOOD
--HERE'S
ONE.

FIRE!

FIRE AND DESTRUCTION!

KASSANDRA!

YOU'LL KILL US ALL!

WHAT'S HAPPENING? WHAT'S WRONG WITH HER?

DON'T WORRY, HELEN. SHE HAS FITS SOMETIMES. SHE DID THE SAME THING WHEN I FIRST--

AND YOU! PLUCKED FROM YOUR ROUNDED HUSK TO LEAD THE SCALY SERPENT ACROSS THE FLOOD!

STOP THAT NOISE AT ONCE, KASSANDRA! I'LL HAVE YOU HAULED OUT--

OH, MY CITY! WOE! WOE! FOUNDED ON THE HILL OF DOOM!

HEKTOR, POLYDAMAS --WOULD YOU ESCORT KASSANDRA OUTSIDE?

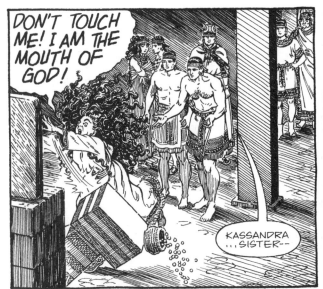

DON'T TOUCH ME! I AM THE MOUTH OF GOD!

KASSANDRA ...SISTER--

NO! I HAVE ONLY **ONE** BROTHER--

HELENUS!

MY **TRUE** BROTHER--GROWING TOGETHER IN MOTHER'S WOMB --ONE BIRTH--ONE MIND--YOU **KNOW** THE GOD'S WORDS ARE **TRUE**--

UHHH...

DEATH HOVERS OVER TROY-- **TELL THEM!** YOU **KNOW** IT! YOU **SEE** IT!

NO-- I CAN'T --I DON'T--

HELENUS, DON'T-- DON'T DO THIS TO ME -- NOT AGAIN-- DON'T LEAVE ME TO STRUGGLE ALONE--NOT LIKE THAT DAY --THE DAY WE NEVER SPEAK OF--

THAT CURSE HAS LINGERED EVER SINCE --LIKE THE TASTE OF HIS SALIVA IN MY MOUTH. BUT YOU ESCAPED THE CURSE, MY BROTHER, MY TWIN, MY UNCURSED SELF.

TELL THEM! *TELL THEM!* THEY'LL *BELIEVE* YOU! *TELL THEM!*

UNH!

KASSANDRA...

HELENUS! DON'T DESERT ME!

KASSANDRA...

NOAAAAAAAAAAAAAAAAAAAAAA

CONFINE HER TO HER ROOM. IDAEUS, I WANT SOMEONE WATCHING HER DAY AND NIGHT.

YES, GREAT KING.

≥AHUH≤
≥HAAH≤
≥KAH≤
≥AHUH≤

PEOPLE OF TROY, WE ARE HERE TO FULFILL A DECREE OF THE GODS--A SACRED UNION--

--WHICH MARKS THE START OF THE WEDDING FEAST!

THAT NIGHT.

...UNWATERED WINE, SO NOW ALL THE WATCHMEN ARE DRUNK ON DUTY.

AND PEOPLE WONDER WHY I DISLIKE FEASTS! WELL, ROUSE THE NEXT WATCH. THE DRUNKARDS WILL BE WHIPPED IN THE MORNING.

AND IF ANY HINT OF THIS REACHES PRIAM, I'LL HAVE *YOU* WHIPPED, TOO!

--SO HE GETS THIS HIGH AND MIGHTY LOOK ON HIS FACE AND SAYS THAT AS KING OF EGYPT HE'LL *KEEP* HELEN AND ALL OUR SHIPS AND TREASURE UNTIL HE CAN SEND FOR *MENELAUS.*

WHAT? YOU'RE JOKING!

BUT HOW DID HE KNOW WHO YOU ARE?

HA! YOU WON'T BELIEVE THIS! AT SIDON, WE RAIDED SOME EGYPTIAN MERCHANT SHIPS. BUT THEIR CAPTAIN ESCAPED. WHEN WE REACHED EGYPT, I THOUGHT IT WOULD BE A GOOD JOKE TO INCLUDE GOODS FROM THOSE SHIPS AMONG THE GIFTS WE PRESENTED TO THE KING. BUT THE SHIPS' CAPTAIN WAS *THERE*--AT THE KING'S COURT!

HE SHRIEKED AND SPLUTTERED TO THE KING WHO WE WERE AND WHAT WE'D DONE. THE KING STAYED CALM, BUT THOSE PAINTED EYES OF HIS BORING INTO HELEN DIDN'T FOOL ME. HE WASN'T ABOUT TO SEND FOR MENELAUS. HE MAY BE THE KING OF EGYPT, BUT HE'S ALSO A *MAN!*

SO HOW'D YOU GET AWAY?

I WENT--I MEAN, I *SENT* BACK TO THE SHIPS TO GET ONE OF THE WOMEN I CAPTURED IN SIDON--ABOUT HELEN'S SIZE AND BUILD--

ALL RIGHT, I'LL ADMIT IT-- I'M AS UNEASY AS THE REST OF YOU. BUT IT'S TOO LATE NOW.

PRIAM JUST SHOULDN'T HAVE WELCOMED HER.

AND THE WAY HE KEEPS TOUCHING HER EVERY CHANCE HE GETS. IT'S UNSEEMLY.

YES, I'LL MENTION THAT PRIVATELY TO HIM. BUT YOU KNOW PRIAM AND EXOTIC WOMEN...

I WISH YOU'D TALK HIM INTO SENDING HER BACK TO SPARTA. THE ACHAEANS AREN'T IGNORING THIS, SO RUMOR SAYS.

EVEN THOUGH WE'RE PERFECTLY JUSTIFIED IN KEEPING HER--REVENGE FOR PAST WRONGS--HESIONE AND ALL THAT.

HMF-- WE ALL KNOW THERE'S MORE TO HESIONE THAN PRIAM LIKES TO ADMIT...

BUT WILL THE ACHAEANS DARE ATTACK TROY? THEY'D LOSE MORE THAN HELEN--TRADE ROUTES, RELATIONS WITH OUR ALLIES, STATUS AMONG PEOPLES--

ONLY IF THEY LOSE, POLYDAMAS. REPORTS SAY THEY'VE ALREADY RAISED AN ARMY LARGER THAN THE WORLD HAS EVER SEEN BEFORE.

THOSE REPORTS ARE CERTAINLY EXAGGERATED, ANTENOR. ACHAEA'S BARELY CIVILIZED.

I HOPE YOU'RE RIGHT, THYMOETES. BUT I FEAR FOR TROY.

SEND HER BACK. IT'S THE ONLY WAY.

THE DAMAGE IS DONE, PANTHOUS--THE ACHAEANS HAVE THEIR EXCUSE TO ATTACK US. LET'S STOP OUR GRUMBLING AND PREPARE TO DEFEND OUR CITY.

I CAN'T BELIEVE THAT BUMPKIN GOT SO LUCKY.

WHAT'S THE MATTER, DEIPHOBUS? JEALOUS?

HMF.

WHO *WOULDN'T* BE JEALOUS?

HEY, *I'M* JEALOUS!

JUST *LOOK* AT THAT BODY.

WHO CAN *STOP* LOOKING?

IF *I* HAD HER, WE'D BE DOING IT ALL DAY AND ALL NIGHT.

HEY! HA HA!

SHUT UP, MESTOR! THE ONLY WAY *YOU'LL* EVER DO IT IS WITH YOUR *HAND!*

YOU'RE THE ONE WHO BETTER KEEP HIS HAND IN SHAPE! *YOU'LL* NEVER GET *HER* AWAY FROM PARIS!

CHILDREN...

WHERE'RE YOU GOING?

OFF TO HAND-PRACTICE? FFT-FFT-FFT!

COME ON, DEIPHOBUS, CALM DOWN.

GROW UP, MESTOR!

ANH!

HE'S GOT IT *BAD!*

DEIPHOBUS, CAUGHT IN THE COILS OF LOVE!

I DON'T BELIEVE IT!

YOU CAN PRACTICALLY SEE THE RING IN HIS NOSE!

YOU'RE ONE TO TALK, HELIKAON-- SNARED BY LAODIKE!

IF WE FREE MEN DON'T KEEP VIGILANT, THERE WON'T BE ANY OF US LEFT-- RIGHT, TROILUS?

HUNH? OH... RIGHT...

IT'S...IT'S SO HOT IN HERE...

CRESSIDA?

HA HA HA HA HA...

CRESSIDA, IT'S TIME TO GO HOME NOW.

BUT, UNCLE, IT'S SUCH A BEAUTIFUL NIGHT-- MAKES EVERYTHING SEEM...SO SMALL...

HA HA ha ha ha...

MF!

STUPID-- STUPID-- STUPID!

GATHER AROUND, EVERYONE. FILL YOUR CUPS, AND LET'S DRINK TO PARIS, PRINCE OF TROY, AND HIS BRIDE, HELEN!

HELEN, BEFORE I SAW YOU, I DOUBTED THE WISDOM OF BRINGING YOU INTO TROY.

BUT NOW THAT YOU'RE HERE, IT'S OBVIOUS--TO *EVERYONE*--THAT YOU BELONG. SO HERE YOU'LL STAY.

IF ANYONE TRIES TO TAKE YOU AWAY, TROY WILL BE YOUR SHIELD. WE'LL MEET ALL OPPOSITION WITH COURAGE.

YOUR ENEMIES ARE TROY'S ENEMIES. TROY'S ALLIES ARE YOUR ALLIES.

THIS IS THE GODS' WILL.

IT IS ALSO MY PLEASURE.

NOW, DRINK!

GREAT KING--

WOULDN'T THIS BE A GOOD MOMENT TO DRINK TO ANOTHER WOMAN AS WELL? ONE WHO ISN'T A WIFE YET, BUT SOON WILL BE--YOUR DAUGHTER, KREUSA--

AENEAS, TONIGHT IS FOR PARIS AND HELEN.

BUT, GREAT KING, KREUSA'S AND MY JOY CAN'T DETRACT FROM THEIRS-- ONLY ADD TO IT.

ISN'T THAT TRUE, PARIS?

YAAAOHHHH-- IT'S LATE-- COME ON, HELEN...

HELEN-- PARIS, WAIT.

I'D LIKE TO, GREAT KING. BUT I WANT TO SHOW HELEN THE SUNRISE. GOODNIGHT, EVERYONE.

GREAT KING--

AENEAS, YOU PRESUME TOO FAR. I HAVEN'T GIVEN MY DAUGHTER TO YOU YET.

I BROUGHT PARIS SAFELY BACK. YOUR PROMISE--

I CHARGED YOU WITH GUIDING PARIS IN HIS UNDERTAKING. HE FAILED, AND NOW WE'RE STARING INTO THE FACE OF WAR WITH THE ACHAEANS. YOU HAVEN'T EARNED MY DAUGHTER.

IF YOU'RE RIGHT-- IF WAR COMES TO TROY--DON'T LOOK FOR HELP FROM *DARDANIA*.

AENEAS--

STAY WHERE YOU ARE, KREUSA!

NO, HEKUBA, DON'T PLEAD FOR HER--I WON'T LISTEN, EVEN TO YOU.

NOT FOR *HER*...

FOR ME.

TONIGHT I WANT TO FEEL LIKE A NEWLYWED WOMAN ONCE MORE...

"STARING INTO THE FACE OF WAR"? PRIAM ISN'T GIVEN TO EXAGGERATION.

HE WAS ANGRY, HE'D DRUNK A LOT OF WINE, AND HE SUSPECTS THE DARDANIAN BRANCH OF THE FAMILY OF COVETING THE THRONE. STILL, I FEAR HE'S CLOSER TO THE TRUTH THAN ANY OF US REALIZES.

ISN'T THAT THE BOWL KREUSA WAS CARRYING?

THAT'S ODD--SHE WAS JUST HERE A MOMENT AGO. IT'S LIKE THE EARTH SWALLOWED HER UP.

COME ON. I WANT YOU TO SEE THIS.

SEE? EVERYONE'S CELEBRATING. THE WHOLE CITY'S LIT UP JUST FOR *YOU*.

IT'S SO MUCH MORE THAN I EVER...

YOU'LL BE QUEEN OF IT ALL THE DAY I BECOME KING.

DREAMER. PRIAM INTENDS HEKTOR TO SUCCEED HIM.

UHH... RIGHT.

WELL, WHO CARES ABOUT BEING KING?

I HAVE *OTHER* INTERESTS...

ENH?

UHH...

HELEN...
HELEN,
WAKE
UP.

NNUH?

WE'RE MISSING THE
SUNRISE!

OHH--I'M
STIFF...

IT'S
BRIGHT!

PARIS,
LOOK!

I'VE NEVER SEEN FOG LIKE *THIS* BEFORE!

THERE'S BARELY ANY WIND.

IT'S ALL AROUND-- EVERY DIRECTION.

IT'S AS IF WE'RE THE ONLY PEOPLE LEFT IN THE ENTIRE WORLD.

LOOK! I WONDER WHAT IT MEANS.

A SWAN. I NEVER LEARNED TO READ BIRD FLIGHTS.

A SWAN.

WHEN I WAS LITTLE, MY MOTHER TOLD ME I HATCHED FROM A SWAN'S EGG. I BELIEVED HER UNTIL I GREW OLD ENOUGH TO KNOW BETTER.

THEN SHE SAID THAT THE THUNDER GOD HAD COME TO HER AS A SWAN AND THAT I WAS THEIR OFFSPRING. I *WANTED* TO BELIEVE THAT, BUT I DIDN'T REALLY.

INSTEAD, *SHE* STARTED BELIEVING IT. SHE DIDN'T TELL ME MUCH OF ANYTHING AFTER THAT-- MY FATHER STARTED TO KEEP HER AWAY FROM PEOPLE...

...I WONDER WHETHER ANYONE HAS TOLD HER I LEFT SPARTA.

HELLO-O-O-O-O...

ACHILLES, ARE YOU GOING TO STARE INTO THE FOG ALL DAY?

LAST NIGHT AT COUNCIL WHEN MENELAUS SAID OUR DAYS OF SAILING WOULD END TODAY AT TROY, I DECIDED MY SHIPS WOULD LAUNCH *FIRST* AT DAWN.

BUT THIS *FOG*... THIS *DRIFTING*...

HELLO-O-O-O...

HELLO-O-O-O...

HELLO-O-O-O...

FETCH MORE WINE, AUTOMEDON. I'LL OFFER YET *ANOTHER* LIBATION TO THE SUN GOD --NO! THIS TIME TO THE GOD OF FIRE --TO *BURN* THIS FOG AWAY!

WHY NOT TO YOUR GRANDFATHER, THE SEA--TO CARRY US TO LAND? *ANY* LAND.

THE ONLY LAND *I* WANT TO SEE IS TROY.

HELLO-O-O-O!

HELLO-O-O-O... HELLO-O-O-O... HELLO-O-O-O... HELLO-O-O-O...

HELLO-O-O-O!

HERE'S THE WINE, ACHILLES.

HELLO-O-O-O...

HELLO-O-O-O...

HELLO-O-O-O...

ACHILLES?

THERE!

HELLO-O-O-O...

DO YOU SEE IT?

LAND!

I DON'T...

IDENTIFY YOURSELVES!

COME NO FARTHER! OR IN THE NAME OF TELEPHUS OF MYSIA, WE'LL DRIVE YOU AWAY! WHO ARE YOU?

WE ARE YOUR DEATH, TROJANS! WE ARE REVENGE!

TURN AROUND AND GO! THIS IS YOUR ONLY WARNING!

CHUK!

TOO MANY OF 'EM! NEED MORE MEN!

TELL KING TELEPHUS!

RUN! RU-- GGGAAAUCK-K-K...

TELEPHUS?

HIERA. NOT NOW. PIRATES ARE ATTACKING THE COAST.

IF THEY'RE AS NUMEROUS AS REPORTED, YOU WILL NEED MANY WARRIORS TO DRIVE THEM AWAY.

YES, EVERY SHEPHERD, EVERY FARMER, EVERY FARMER'S *SON*--

ALL WHO CAN SWING CLUBS OR THROW STONES, BUT TRAINED *WARRIORS* ARE SCARCE IN MYSIA.

I'LL LEAD THE CHARIOTS, TEUTHRANIUS COMMANDS THE ARCHERS, AND--

AND I WILL LEAD MY--

YOU? YOU'LL STAY *HERE*--

DO YOU FORGET, TELEPHUS? BEFORE I CAME HERE TO BE YOUR WIFE, I WAS A WARRIOR-PRINCESS ALONG THE BLACK SEA COAST. THE MEN AND WOMEN WHO CAME HERE WITH ME WERE MY ARMY. TIME AND AGAIN WE TURNED BACK PIRATES FROM OUR SHORES. LET US SHOW YOU THAT WE ARE STILL WARRIORS.

HIERA...YOU'RE NO LONGER A WARRIOR-PRINCESS. YOU'RE MY WIFE. GO AND WAIT WITH MY OTHER WIVES FOR MY RETURN FROM BATTLE.

AND IF YOU *DO NOT* RETURN?

THEN BURN MY BODY WITH ALL THE HONOR AN EXCELLENT WIFE OWES HER KING AND HUSBAND.

ODYSSEUS! THIS ISN'T ≡HEM≡ THIS ISN'T **TROY**!

WE'LL SORT THAT OUT LATER, KALCHAS! RIGHT NOW IT'S A **BATTLE**!

AJAX! THERSANDER'S DEAD-- MANY OTHERS DEAD OR WOUNDED! IF WE DON'T RALLY, WE'LL BE PUSHED BACK TO THE SHIPS!

TAKE YOUR MEN TO THE NORTH END OF THE BATTLE, ACHILLES. I'LL LEAD A FRONTAL ATTACK. WE'LL DRIVE THE TROJANS TO THE HELLESPONT. THEN WITH FRESH MEN FROM THE SHIPS STILL LANDING, WE'LL EASILY--

AJAX! LOOK OUT!

AAA
AAGH!

ACHILLES! TROJAN CHARIOTS!

ACHILLES!

THEY AREN'T PURSUING.

NO...IT'S GETTING ...TOO DARK ...FOR ANY ...MORE... FIGHTING...

--OHHhhh...

PATROKLUS!

MY ARM...

HOLD STILL-- I'LL PULL THE ARROW OUT.

ANH!

YOUR ARM'S WOUNDED **TWICE**.

YES--AAH-- THE ARROW --AND THAT SPEAR BEFORE.

OH. YES, THAT'S RIGHT...BOTH TIMES COMING TO **MY** AID.

THERE. WE, UH..., WE SHOULD GET TO THE SHIPS. YOUR ARM NEEDS A HONEY POULTICE.

ACHILLES...

WHAT?

NOTHING...

PATROKLUS, I--

LISTEN TO ME, PATROKLUS...

I VOW TO ACCOMPANY YOU IN BATTLE-- **ALWAYS.** I'LL NEVER BE FAR FROM YOUR SIDE. WE'LL STAND TOGETHER AND MEET THE ENEMY AS ONE! IN THE NAMES OF ALL THE GODS, I PROMISE YOU.

THAT'S ...VERY GENEROUS. AND NOBLE. I PROMISE TO ALWAYS STAND BESIDE YOU TOO, ACHILLES.

YES, UH... THAT'S GOOD. THAT'S GOOD TO KNOW.

WELL, THE BLEEDING'S STOPPED. I SUPPOSE WE SHOULD GET GOING. COULD YOU...COULD YOU HELP ME STAND?

YES, YES, CERTAINLY...

OH, THANK THE GODS--

PATROKLUS IS WOUNDED. HE NEEDS A PHYSICIAN RIGHT AWAY.

THEY'RE TENDING THE WOUNDED ALONG THAT WAY, BY THE SHIPS FROM TRIKKA. BUT--

AUTOMEDON, DRIVE THERE.

ACHILLES, HIGH KING AGAMEMNON WANTS TO SEE YOU *NOW*.

NOT YET, PHOENIX.

FIRST I NEED TO MAKE SURE THAT PATROKLUS IS CARED FOR.

AUTOMEDON CAN SEE TO PATROKLUS. THE HIGH KING IS IN *NO* MOOD FOR DELAY...

CAN'T YOU DRIVE FASTER, AUTOMEDON?

ACHILLES! YOU'RE SUPPOSED TO FOLLOW MY ADVICE. YOUR FATHER--

HAA!

I WILL, PHOENIX. AFTER-WARD!

ACHILLES, I DON'T THINK YOU REALIZE WHAT'S HAPPENED-- WHERE WE ARE! *ACHILLES!*

HERE HE IS AT LAST, HIGH KING.

PHOENIX, THANK YOU.

ACHILLES, SON OF PELEUS, I'M TOLD THAT YOUR SHIPS WERE THE FIRST TO LAND, THAT YOU WERE THE FIRST TO ENGAGE IN BATTLE.

YES, HIGH KING, I WAS THE FIRST FROM OUR ARMY... THE *TROJANS* THREW THE FIRST SPEAR.

NO, THEY DIDN'T. THIS ISN'T TROY. THOSE MEN AREN'T TROJANS. YOU'VE DRAWN US INTO A WAR THAT'S NOT SUPPOSED TO BE HAPPENING.

WHAT? I--

...BUT WHY BLAME *ME*? *EVERYONE* ELSE SAID THIS WAS TROY! IT *LOOKS* LIKE MENELAUS'S DESCRIPTIONS--

MY DESCRIPTIONS? WHERE IS THE RICH CITY OVERLOOKING THE PLAIN? THE TWO RIVERS FLOWING INTO THE BAY? THE SWIFT HELLESPONT TO THE NORTH? IS *THIS* A PLACE THAT WOULD LURE A KING'S WIFE?

ENOUGH! *I* LED THE ACHAEANS INTO BATTLE -- I ACCEPT RESPONSIBILITY FOR THE MISTAKE. BUT WHAT'S DONE IS DONE. IN THE MORNING, LET'S GET BACK INTO OUR SHIPS AND GO. LET MENELAUS TAKE THE LEAD--OR SOMEONE ELSE WHO'S BEEN TO TROY --SO THAT NO ONE MAKES ANOTHER MISTAKE.

THE FLEET CAN'T SAIL SO QUICKLY. HUNDREDS OF OUR MEN ARE DEAD, AND MANY MORE ARE WOUNDED.

THERSANDER OF THEBES FELL TODAY. HE WAS A GREAT WARRIOR AND KING, SO HE MUST HAVE A FUNERAL AND GAMES.

WE'LL BE DELAYED HERE FOR *DAYS*, RECOVERING--AND THAT'S AS LONG AS THE LOCALS DON'T ATTACK AGAIN!

AND LOOK AT OUR MEN--

--THEY'VE SUFFERED YEARS OF HARDSHIP AND WAITING FOR THIS WAR. WE COAXED THEM WITH TROJAN RICHES, BOUND THEM WITH OATHS, WHIPPED THEM INTO SUBMISSION--

--ONLY TO LEAD THEM HERE TO A WAR NO ONE WANTS. WE'RE NOT *LEADING*, WE'RE *BUMBLING*--

PALAMEDES! THAT'S *ENOUGH!*

AT FIRST LIGHT, I'LL SEND ENVOYS TO THE LOCAL KING TO ARRANGE A TRUCE TO COLLECT AND BURY THE DEAD.

OUR GOAL REMAINS THE SAME -- TO TAKE TROY.

ACHILLES, WE ALL REALIZE YOU'RE YOUNG AND INEXPERIENCED. BUT MISTAKES SUCH AS YOURS TODAY ARE COSTLY. DON'T MAKE ANOTHER.

YES, HIGH KING.

NEXT DAY.

...IT SEEMS SO WRONG TO BURY HIM SO FAR FROM HIS FOREFATHERS, HIGH KING.

EVEN IF YOU SAILED IMMEDIATELY, PENELEOS, THE BODY COULDN'T REACH THEBES BEFORE THE DECAY BECAME SO GREAT--

I KNOW. I KNOW.

BUT LEAVING THERSANDER HERE ON A FOREIGN SHORE --A SHORE WE DON'T EVEN KNOW THE NAME OF...

I THINK WE'LL LEARN THE ANSWER TO THAT RIGHT NOW. MY ENVOYS ARE BACK.

WHAT'S YOUR REPORT, TALTHYBIUS?

FIRST, HIGH KING, WE HAVE A NINE DAY TRUCE.

VERY GOOD.

SECOND, WE ARE IN THE LAND OF MYSIA, IN THE AREA CALLED TEUTHRANIA. THE KING OF MYSIA IS TELEPHUS--

TELEPHUS?

TELEPHUS, SON OF HERAKLES?

I BELIEVE SO, THOUGH WE WEREN'T GRANTED AN AUDIENCE WITH HIM.

I'M A SON OF HERAKLES, TOO, HIGH KING. TELEPHUS IS MY BROTHER. NEVER MET HIM, BUT I THINK I CAN ARRANGE A PERMANENT TRUCE.

JUST WHAT WE WANT, TLEPOLEMUS, THE SOONER, THE BETTER. TALTHYBIUS WILL TAKE YOU RIGHT NOW.

TALTHYBIUS, DO WHATEVER IT TAKES TO ARRANGE AN AUDIENCE FOR TLEPOLEMUS WITH THIS KING TELEPHUS. AND TAKE ANTIPHUS AND PHIDIPPUS ALONG--THEY'RE GRANDSONS OF HERAKLES.

YES, HIGH KING.

ANTIPHUS AND PHIDIPPUS --GOOD IDEA!

TLEPOLEMUS, ONE MORE THING-- PERSUADE THIS TELEPHUS TO JOIN US AGAINST TROY. WE'VE LOST HUNDREDS OF MEN HERE AND NEED REINFORCEMENTS --AND WE WANT THE MYSIAN ARMY FIGHTING *WITH* US --NOT *AGAINST* US.

SHOULD BE EASY. WE'RE BOTH SONS OF HERAKLES.

BOTH SONS OF HERAKLES... YOU'LL EITHER FALL INTO EACH OTHER'S ARMS OR YOU'LL KILL EACH OTHER.

HA!

APPROACH THE THRONE OF TELEPHUS, THE KING OF MYSIA.

WHO ARE YOU AND WHAT DO YOU WANT?

YOU'RE TELEPHUS WHOM AUGE OF TEGEA BORE TO HERAKLES?

YES. DON'T TEST MY PATIENCE. YOU'VE SLAIN HUNDREDS OF MY PEOPLE. MY GREATEST WARRIORS LIE DEAD--HAIMOS AND MY BROTHER TEUTHRANIUS. SO DOES HIERA, MY WIFE. I'VE AGREED TO YOUR TRUCE-- WHAT MORE DO YOU WANT?

IN OUR FATHER'S NAME AND BY ALL THE GODS, I DECLARE THAT I AM TLEPOLEMUS, KING OF RHODES, WHOM ASTYOCHEA OF EPHYRA BORE TO HERAKLES.

I AM PHIDIPPUS, KING OF KOS. MY FATHER WAS THESSALUS, WHOM CHALKIOPE OF KOS BORE TO HERAKLES.

THIS IS MY BROTHER, ANTIPHUS, ALSO A GRANDSON OF HERAKLES.

YES, I KNEW HIM. I GREW UP IN HIS PALACE AT ARGOS. I SAW HIM MANY TIMES BEFORE HE BECAME A GOD.

BRING SEATS FOR MY GUESTS--AND FOOD AND WINE.

ANTIPHUS AND I DIDN'T KNOW OUR GRANDFATHER, BUT WE NEVER GET TIRED OF HEARING STORIES ABOUT HIM.

YOU SHOULD TALK TO SOME OF THE OTHER ACHAEAN CHIEFS WHO KNEW HIM --PHILOKTETES, NESTOR...

EXCELLENT! IN TWELVE DAYS --AFTER THE FUNERALS--I INVITE EVERYONE WHO'S KIN TO HERAKLES OR WHO KNEW HIM TO FEAST WITH ME IN MY HALL.

THAT'LL BE A WELCOME CHANGE AFTER OUR SEA JOURNEY AND YESTERDAY'S FIGHTING. YOU KNOW, BROTHER, AS AN ACHAEAN YOURSELF, YOU OUGHT TO JOIN US.

JOIN YOU IN WHAT? PIRATE RAIDS?

NO, IT'S A LONG STORY.

A PRINCE OF TROY NAMED PARIS WAS A GUEST OF MENELAUS OF LAKEDAEMON. BUT THIS PARIS LOOTED MENELAUS'S PALACE AND CARRIED OFF HIS WIFE. YOU MIGHT HAVE HEARD OF HER-- HELEN, DAUGHTER OF TYNDAREUS.

AH, THE BEAUTY BEYOND COMPARE. I REMEMBER ALL OF THE ACHAEAN KINGS TRYING TO OUTDO ONE ANOTHER TO WIN HER. THAT'S ABOUT THE TIME I LEFT TEGEA TO SEARCH FOR MY MOTHER.

NOW HELEN'S SUITORS HAVE BANDED TOGETHER UNDER THE SONS OF ATREUS, MENELAUS AND HIGH KING AGAMEMNON. WE'RE OFF TO ATTACK TROY AND RESCUE HELEN. YOUR ARMY WOULD--

STOP!

DON'T ASK ME TO JOIN YOU.

 I JUST THOUGHT-- WELL, OUR ARMY IS DECIMATED. YOUR MYSIANS MIGHT FILL THE PLACES OF THOSE THEY KILLED OR WOUNDED.

I WILL MAKE WHAT REPARATIONS I CAN. I INVITE ALL OF YOU WHO ARE MY KINSMEN TO FEAST WITH ME. I'LL HAVE YOUR WOUNDED ESCORTED SOUTH TO THE HOT SPRINGS TO RECOVER. I'LL EVEN PROVISION YOUR FLEET. BUT DON'T ASK ME TO JOIN YOU AGAINST TROY.

 LET ME REMIND YOU THAT OUR FATHER, HERAKLES, ONCE SACKED TROY. ARE YOU HINTING THAT FOLLOWING HIS EXAMPLE IS WRONG?

 YOU DON'T KNOW WHAT YOU'RE ASKING.

THAT WOMAN IS MY WIFE, ASTYOCHE. SHE'S A SISTER OF PRIAM, KING OF TROY. THE BOY IS OUR SON EURYPYLUS. I WILL NOT--I *CAN NOT* ATTACK MY SON'S FAMILY.

A MOMENT AGO YOU ACCUSED ME OF HOSTILITY TO MY ACHAEAN KINSMEN--DON'T ASK ME TO BE HOSTILE TO MY TROJAN KINSMEN.

 AH, HERE'S THE WINE. LET'S TALK ABOUT SOMETHING OTHER THAN TROY--TELL ME ABOUT HERAKLES.

ALL RIGHT. HMM.

 FOR ONE THING, YOU LOOK A LOT LIKE HIM.

OUR FATHERS WERE CLOSE FRIENDS. HERAKLES PRAYED TO ZEUS THAT MY MOTHER WOULD BEAR A SON, AND SO I WAS BORN. THEN HERAKLES WRAPPED ME IN HIS LION SKIN, AND THAT MADE ME HARD TO KILL.

MY MOTHER HESIONE IS YOUR WIFE ASTYOCHE'S SISTER. MY BROTHER AJAX AND I PRESENT YOU WITH THIS FINE CLOAK WOVEN BY MY MOTHER.

THANK YOU, SONS OF TELAMON. WELCOME TO MYSIA.

THIS IS ACHILLES OF PHTHIA, WHOM THE SEA-NYMPH THETIS BORE TO PELEUS THE ARGONAUT.

I'M NOT CLOSELY RELATED TO HERAKLES, BUT WHEN I LEARNED THAT THE KING OF MYSIA WAS HIS SON, I REMEMBERED THE MYSIAN WARRIOR WHO WORE A LION SKIN.

HONOR DEMANDS THAT I OFFER MY GRAVEST REGRETS FOR LEADING THE ATTACK AND WOUNDING YOU. I CAN'T TAKE BACK MY SPEAR THRUST, BUT THIS SALVE -- PREPARED BY THE KENTAUR WHO TAUGHT ME HEALING -- WILL SOOTHE THE WOUND.

THANK YOU, ACHILLES. IN THE RUSH TO BATTLE, I FORGOT THE SACRIFICE TO THE GOD OF WINE, SO HE TRIPPED ME WITH A VINE. OTHERWISE, YOU'D NEVER HAVE TOUCHED ME.

STILL, I'M SURE IT'S PAINFUL. IF YOU'LL STAND, I CAN APPLY THE SALVE.

NO, NO... THAT'S NOT NECESSARY -- I MUST CONTINUE TO GREET MY GUESTS.

IT'S ALL RIGHT. I'M THE LAST ONE. IS IT TOO PAINFUL TO STAND? LET ME TAKE A LOOK.

OH!

THE LAST ONE? BUT WHERE ARE THE SONS OF ATREUS--AGAMEMNON AND MENELAUS?

YOUR WOUND NEEDS IMMEDIATE TREATMENT, BUT IT'S BEYOND MY SKILL.

THEY MUST COME TO MY FEAST. THEY'RE THE LEADERS OF YOUR ARMY AS WELL AS MY COUSINS.

ODYSSEUS, COULD YOU RETURN TO CAMP AND GET MACHAON AND PODALIRIUS?

NO, NO, HE MEANS AGAMEMNON AND MENELAUS.

NO, HE NEEDS THE PHYSICIANS URGENTLY. LOOK!

EHHH...

I AM NOT A SPECTACLE! I HAVE MY OWN HEALERS!

WITHOUT TREATMENT THIS WILL KILL YOU!

LET'S STAY CALM. I'LL BRING AGAMEMNON AND MENELAUS BACK WITH ME IF YOU'LL AGREE TO LET MACHAON AND PODALIRIUS TREAT YOUR WOUND.

THERE AREN'T BETTER HEALERS IN THE WORLD. THEY'RE SONS OF THE GREAT PHYSICIAN ASKLEPIUS. HE'S WORSHIPPED AS A GOD --JUST LIKE YOUR FATHER, HERAKLES.

ALL RIGHT. ALL RIGHT. BRING THEM ALL -- I HAVE PLENTY OF FOOD AND WINE TO GO AROUND.

WHY SHOULD I BE BOTHERED WITH SOME BACK-COUNTRY EXCUSE FOR A FEAST? WE SHOULDN'T EVEN *BE* IN MYSIA!

BUT WE *ARE* HERE, AND YOU'RE HIS COUSIN. HE EXPECTS YOU TO ACCEPT HIS HOSPITALITY. YOU'LL *INSULT* HIM IF YOU DON'T.

SO THE HIGH KING OF MYCENAE IS SUPPOSED TO BOW TO THE WISHES OF A PETTY LOCAL RULER WHO REFUSES TO JOIN US AGAINST TROY?

WELL, YOU CERTAINLY WON'T PERSUADE HIM TO JOIN US IF YOU WON'T EVEN SPEAK TO HIM.

ODYSSEUS HAS A POINT, AGAMEMNON. AND IF WE INSULT HIM BY STAYING HERE IN CAMP, WE JUST GIVE HIM MORE IMPETUS TO JOIN THE TROJANS.

HE'S SERVING ROASTED BOAR...

WHY ARE YOU TAKING MACHAON AND PODALIRIUS? THEY'RE NEEDED HERE.

ACHILLES WOUNDED TELEPHUS IN THE BATTLE. THEY'RE GOING TO HEAL HIM.

IT'LL PUT TELEPHUS FURTHER INTO OUR DEBT.

ODYSSEUS, YOU'RE TOO CLEVER. WAIT WHILE I SCRAPE TOGETHER SOME APPROPRIATE GIFTS. WE BETTER DRESS, TOO, MENELAUS. CAN'T RISK BEING OUTSHONE BY THE LOCALS.

SEVEN DAYS LATER.

A FINE DAY FOR SAILING, AGAMEMNON. FOLLOW MY DIRECTIONS, AND YOUR FLEET WILL HAVE NO TROUBLE FINDING AND RECOGNIZING TROY.

JUST TO BE DOUBLY SURE, ODYSSEUS LEADS THE FLEET WITH THE FORMER TROJAN, KALCHAS, BY HIS SIDE.

AND TO BE *TRIPLY* SURE, MY SHIPS WILL SAIL CLOSE BEHIND ODYSSEUS'S. WE WON'T MISS TROY THIS TIME.

NOW WE'VE GOT TO BE OFF, TELEPHUS, BUT BEFORE WE LEAVE, I'LL ASK YOU ONE LAST TIME TO JOIN US AGAINST TROY.

I'VE PROVIDED YOU WITH HOSPITALITY, PROVISIONED YOUR FLEET, GIVEN YOU DIRECTIONS AND EXPLAINED THE BEST LANDING PLACE AT TROY. EVEN NOW I PRESENT YOU WITH THESE PRECIOUS GOODS AS PARTING GIFTS.

BUT YOU *KNOW* WHY I CAN'T JOIN YOU, AGAMEMNON. DON'T ASK ME AGAIN.

THEN I THANK YOU FOR YOUR HOSPITALITY, YOUR GIFTS, AND YOUR ADVICE. MAY THE GODS BLESS YOU WHENEVER YOU REMEMBER THEM IN PRAYER.

AND MAY THEY GRANT YOU A SAFE VOYAGE.

BEFORE I DEPART, I WANT TO MAKE SURE YOUR WOUND IS HEALING PROPERLY.

YOU SEE ME STANDING, DON'T YOU, MACHAON? YOU AND YOUR BROTHER ARE MARVELOUS.

I WISH THAT WOUND HAD FESTERED AND KILLED HIM.

MACHAON AND PODALIRIUS WOULD *NEVER* HAVE AGREED TO LET THAT HAPPEN.

THAT'S WHY I DIDN'T SUGGEST IT. BUT IT'S ALL I COULD THINK ABOUT THE NIGHT OF THE FEAST.

WELL, IF HE JOINS THE TROJANS, WE'LL JUST SEND TLEPOLEMUS TO CONVINCE HIM OTHERWISE.

TLEPOLEMUS, OF ALL THE THINGS YOUR FLEET CARRIED HERE TO TEUTHRANIA, I'M MOST GRATEFUL FOR THE FAMILY I NEVER KNEW BEFORE, PARTICULARLY YOU, MY NEW BROTHER.

AND I'M GRATEFUL THAT THE GODS BROUGHT ME HERE TO YOU, TELEPHUS. I JUST WISH IT HADN'T BEEN AT THE EXPENSE OF SO MANY OTHERS --TEUTHRANIUS, HIERA...

YES, TOO MANY LOSSES ON BOTH SIDES. I SEE A CEMETARY HAS SPRUNG UP HERE AT THE MOUTH OF THE KAIKOS RIVER WHERE DAYS AGO ONLY SCRUBBY BRUSH GREW.

AND WHO'S BURIAL MOUND IS THAT? ANYONE WITH EYES WILL SEE IT FROM FAR AWAY ON BOTH LAND AND WATER.

THERSANDER OF THEBES LIES UNDER IT.

THE MAN WHO SLEW MY HIERA.

HE WAS WELL-LOVED BY THE THEBANS, A BRAVE AND HONORABLE WARRIOR, AS WELL AS THE SON OF POLYNEIKES, WHOM OEDIPUS FATHERED.

OEDIPUS?

OEDIPUS WHO WAS KING OF THEBES, THE ONE WHO MARRIED HIS MO--

WELL...

...THE SCANDAL'S WELL-KNOWN.

FAREWELL, THEN. TAKE THESE GIFTS WITH YOU.

TELEPHUS, A GREAT WARRIOR'S BURIAL MOUND IS CUSTOMARY. IT'S NOT AN INSULT TO YOU.

MAY THE GODS CARRY YOU SAFELY, TLEPOLEMUS. WHEN WE MEET AGAIN, WE'LL MEET AS FRIENDS AND BROTHERS.

TELEPHUS?

ACHILLES.

I'VE COME TO SAY FAREWELL AND EXPRESS MY REMORSE ONE LAST TIME FOR ALL THE PAIN I'VE CAUSED YOU.

ACHILLES...SO YOUNG YET SO HONORABLE. HOW COULD I HOLD A GRUDGE AGAINST SOMEONE SO READY TO MEND INJURIES?

IT SEEMS THE ONLY WAY--TO ACT SWIFTLY AND SURELY--WHETHER TO WOUND AN ENEMY OR TO SOOTHE A FRIEND. HOW ELSE CAN A MAN LIVE IN THE SIGHT OF THE GODS?

OHHH, THERE ARE AS MANY WAYS TO LIVE AS THERE ARE MEN.

EURYPYLUS, I HOPE YOU'LL GROW UP TO BE AS HONORABLE AS ACHILLES.

YES, FATHER.

AND I HOPE MY SON WILL GROW UP TO BE AS OBEDIENT AS YOURS, TELEPHUS.

HERE'S MY PARTING GIFT-- HORSES AS SWIFT AND SURE AS YOU ARE, ACHILLES. I HOPE YOU HAVE ROOM ON ONE OF YOUR SHIPS?

MY SHIPS SAIL LAST TODAY -- PLENTY OF TIME TO FIND ROOM FOR SUCH A MIGHTY GIFT.

...INTERCEPTED ON THE WAY TO SKYTHIA, CARRYING NEWS THAT THE ACHAEANS PLAN TO ATTACK TROY. BUT IT'S NOT JUST LAKEDAEMON AND MYCENAE, IT'S **ALL** ACHAEA AND THE ISLANDS--CRETE RHODES, ITHAKA!

THEY ATTACKED TEUTHRANIA IN MYSIA FIRST, KILLING MANY WARRIORS AS WELL AS ONE OF THE KING'S WIVES -- ONE WHO **WASN'T** ASTYOCHE.

THEY'RE ATTACKING OUR ALLIES TO WEAKEN AND DEMORALIZE US!

POSSIBLE, EVEN PROBABLE. I'LL BE SENDING OUT MESSENGERS TO ALERT ALL OUR ALLIES AND ASK FOR AID.

MEANWHILE, WE NEED TO STRENGTHEN OUR DEFENSES.

HEKTOR, YOU'LL BE IN CHARGE OF ENSURING THE CITY WALLS ARE IN REPAIR. HELENUS, YOU'LL OVERSEE CLEARING OF THE DEFENSIVE DITCHES.

YES, GREAT KING.

YES, FATHER.

WE--THIS--WHY-- WE MUST SEND HELEN **BACK!**

NO!

SILENCE! WE'RE NOT CONCERNED WITH HELEN RIGHT NOW. WE'RE CONCERNED WITH THE LARGEST ARMY THE WORLD HAS EVER SEEN. WE DON'T KNOW WHEN OR WHERE THEY'LL ATTACK, BUT WE MUST PREPARE FOR ANYTHING.

AGAMEMNON!

I THOUGHT YOU WANTED TO REACH MYCENAE BEFORE WE STOPPED FOR TODAY. BUT IT'S NEARLY SUNSET.

I'D HOPED TO BE HOME IN MYCENAE TONIGHT. BUT HALF THE FLEET LOST SAILS IN THE STORM, AND ROWING ANY FASTER EXHAUSTS THE MEN. WE'LL REACH IT TOMORROW.

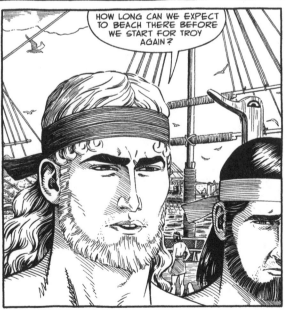

HOW LONG CAN WE EXPECT TO BEACH THERE BEFORE WE START FOR TROY AGAIN?

GO HOME TO SPARTA, MENELAUS. WE'LL SET OUT AGAIN IN THE SPRING.

SPRING! WHY?

MENELAUS, BE PATIENT. THE GODS HAVE PROMISED US VICTORY.

IN TEN YEARS! MEANWHILE MY WIFE AND SON ARE GONE. MY DAUGHTER IS MOTHERLESS. MY WIFE'S PARENTS ARE AGING--

SINCE THAT STORM, WE'RE IN NO SHAPE TO ATTACK TROY. WE DON'T EVEN KNOW WHO'S DROWNED OR BLOWN OFF COURSE OR JUST HEADED HOME LIKE US BECAUSE WHAT ELSE IS THERE TO DO?

I KNOW YOU'D BRAVELY SAIL FOR TROY THIS MOMENT, BUT WHO WOULD JOIN YOU?

THE SUITORS' VOW IS STILL--

LOOK AT THEM. EXHAUSTED. DEMORALIZED. THEY WANT TO GO HOME. THEY WANT TO WALK THROUGH THEIR OWN FIELDS AND SLEEP WITH THEIR OWN WIVES--NOT LIE ON SOME STONY BEACH, PASSING AROUND THE CAMP SLUT.

WHAT ABOUT MY WIFE?

ASK *THEM!* ASK THE *GODS!* *THEY'RE* THE ONES WHO'VE CURSED OUR FAMILY. WE SACRIFICE TO THEM THE BEST OF WHAT WE HAVE, THEN THEY DEMAND EVEN MORE.

AND *I'LL* GIVE IT--*I'LL* WAIT TILL SPRING--I'LL WAIT *TEN YEARS*--WHATEVER THEY ASK, BECAUSE MORE THAN ANY-THING, I WANT TO TAKE TROY. IF YOU WANT YOUR WIFE BACK, *YOU'LL* WAIT, *TOO!*

...MMHHHAA_

--AAOOOH*GODS!*

AAAAAAAAAAAAAAA!

WHAT'S WRONG WITH MENELAUS?

ODYSSEUS, DON'T EVER FALL IN LOVE WITH YOUR WIFE.

WELL, THAT ADVICE IS A BIT LATE. AT FIRST LIGHT I'M SAILING FOR ITHAKA. I'VE COME TO SAY FAREWELL AND TO RETURN KALCHAS TO YOU NOW, SO I WON'T HAVE TO SAIL OUT OF MY WAY TOMORROW.

BUT--ODYSSEUS-- YOU CAN'T JUST GO OFF LIKE THIS...

I HAVEN'T SEEN MY HOME SINCE BEFORE LAST WINTER, AGAMEMNON.

ODYSSEUS, YOU MUST BE MY GUEST AT MYCENAE FOR A FEW WEEKS. I NEED YOUR ASSISTANCE IN PLANNING HOW TO GATHER THE ARMY AGAIN. LOOK HOW DISCOURAGED THEY ALL ARE, AND YOU ALWAYS KNOW JUST THE RIGHT...

HIGH KING, I--

AGAMEMNON! ODYSSEUS!

WHO'LL COME HUNTING WITH US?

HUNTING *NOW*, PALAMEDES? IT'S ALMOST DARK. CAN'T YOU GET BY FOR ONE LAST NIGHT ON PROVISIONS?

THIS MORNING I PROMISED MY MEN WE'D REACH NAUPLIA TODAY. WE DIDN'T MAKE IT, DESPITE ROWING ALL DAY. THEY'RE TIRED AND HOMESICK.

THE LEAST I CAN DO IS TO GIVE THEM FRESH MEAT TONIGHT, EVEN IF IT'S ONLY A BITE OF HARE OR HEDGEHOG. WILL YOU DO THE SAME FOR YOUR MEN?

HUNTING HEDGE-HOGS IN THE DARK...

I HOPE HE TRIPS AND BREAKS HIS NECK.

HOW DOES HE DO IT? CONTINUALLY UNDERMINING MY AUTHORITY WITHOUT EVEN TRYING! THIS IS WHY I NEED YOU AT MYCENAE, ODYSSEUS--TO HELP ME SOLVE *THIS* SORT OF PROBLEM.

IF PALAMEDES IS YOUR PROBLEM, HIGH KING, I'LL BE *HAPPY* TO GIVE YOU A SOLUTION.

YOU CAN'T JUST SPEAR HIM IN THE BACK AND CALL IT A HUNTING ACCIDENT. HE'S MY *COUSIN*, AFTER ALL.

NO, NO. HE'LL MAKE A WRONG STEP EVENTUALLY. THEN WE'LL HAVE HIM. NOTHING THE GODS CAN BLAME US FOR. BUT WE NEED TO BE READY. I'LL ACCOMPANY YOU TO MYCENAE.

MYCENAE.

YES, YES! THAT ONE'S *EXQUISITE*. HURRY-- HE'LL BE CALLING FOR YOU ANY MOMENT.

HMM. NO...

NOT *THAT* ONE-- IT'S COVERED WITH *DIRT*. THERE'S NO TIME TO CLEAN--

DRIED BLOOD. I LAST WORE THIS NECKLACE THE DAY MY FIRST HUSBAND DIED.

TIE IT.

MOTHERRRRR... AREN'T YOU READY *YET*?

BE PATIENT, ELEKTRA. I DON'T WANT TO HEAR ANOTHER WORD.

IPHIGENIA, STOP TUGGING YOUR HAIR, YOU'LL PULL THE CURL OUT.

THERE. MAKE SURE MY SKIRTS ARE SMOOTH IN BACK.

HIGH QUEEN--

ARE THEY IN THE GREAT HALL YET?

THE HIGH KING'S COMPANIONS ARE WAITING THERE, BUT THE HIGH KING IS--

I'M *HERE!*

THERE ARE MY DARLINGS! I WONDERED WHERE YOU WERE HIDING!

WE'VE BEEN WAITING RIGHT HERE, FATHER!

YES!

FAA-DA!

YOU THREE JUST GROW PRETTIER!

EH-HMM...

KLYTEMNESTRA...

AGAMEMNON.

HOW DO YOU EXPECT ME TO GREET YOUR GUESTS IF YOU SPOIL MY HAIR AND MAKE-UP?

THERE'S *PLENTY* OF TIME. ODYSSEUS OF ITHAKA SHOULD BE STAYING FOR *QUITE* AWHILE IF I HAVE MY WAY.

YOU'RE NOT HAVING YOUR WAY *NOW*.

WHAT'S THE MATTER WITH YOU?

YOU--YOU *KNOW* I'M WITH CHILD...

THEN ONE OF THE SERVANT GIRLS WILL HAVE TO DO.

FATHER? I DON'T KNOW WHAT YOU NEED DONE, BUT I'D BE HAPPY TO DO IT FOR YOU--

IPHIGENIA! GO TO YOUR ROOM *AT ONCE!* TAKE YOUR SISTERS WITH YOU!

YES, MOTHER.

OH, GODDESS, PROTECT MY CHILDREN...

AS IF I'D DO ANYTHING TO HURT MY DARLING GIRLS! SHE DIDN'T REALIZE WHAT--

I KNOW WHAT YOU'RE CAPABLE OF! AND I KNOW YOUR *FAMILY HISTORY* AS WELL AS YOU DO!

HAVE A GOOD NIGHT *ALONE!*

WAIT! WHERE'S MY SISTER?

HELEN'S STILL IN TROY.

AH, GODDESS... WE'RE CURSED...

IT'S ATREUS'S SONS WHO ARE CURSED. IT SHOULDN'T TOUCH YOU... OR HELEN.

THERE'S ANOTHER CURSE--THE ONE ON TYNDAREUS'S DAUGHTERS-- MY SISTERS AND ME. WE'RE CURSED TO MARRY AGAIN AND AGAIN... AND TO NEVER BE HAPPY FOR LONG.

WELL, AT LEAST HELEN WILL BE SPARED A LITTLE LONGER FROM LEARNING THAT MOTHER HANGED HERSELF IN DESPAIR OVER HELEN. OH, MOTHER... DEATH CAN'T BE THE *ONLY* ESCAPE.

SKYROS.

PYRRHA!

PYRRHA'S BACK!

ACHILLES!

ACHILLES IS HOME!

PYRRHA!

C'MON, PYRRHA!

IT'S *ACHILLES*!

ACHILLES!

ACHILLES!

LYKOMEDES-- FATHER--WE'VE RETURNED.

ACHILLES, WE HAVEN'T HEARD EVEN ONE WORD OF NEWS ABOUT TROY'S FALL. DON'T TELL US YOU'VE RETURNED TO SKYROS WITHOUT GAINING THE GLORY YOU SOUGHT.

WE WERE...UNSUCCESSFUL. I LOST MEN. BOTH SKYRIANS AND MYRMIDONS FELL IN BATTLE AT MYSIA. THEN A STORM SANK ONE OF THE SHIPS YOU ENTRUSTED TO ME.

UNFORTUNATE. BUT *YOU* SURVIVED. SO WHILE SKYROS MOURNS ITS DEAD, WE'LL HOLD A *PROPER* WEDDING FEAST--UNLIKE THE ONE BEFORE YOUR HASTY DEPARTURE. YOUR COMPANIONS MUST ATTEND.

UH--THE MYRMIDONS WILL SAIL BACK TO PHTHIA TOMORROW. EXCEPT FOR PATROKLUS HERE. HE'LL STAY. WE'RE PLEDGED TO STAND BY EACH OTHER.

ACHILLES...

ACHILLES, AREN'T YOU HAPPY TO BE HOME? IT SEEMS AS IF YOU'VE BEEN GONE FOREVER.

NEOPTOLEMUS! MY HANDSOME BOY!

HEE HEE HEE HAAA!

WE BOTH MISSED YOU SO MUCH!

HA HA HA HEEE!

WHEE!

OH! EXCUSE ME...

HEE HEE

SMACK

OF COURSE, AS LONG AS I HAD NEOPTOLEMUS, IT WAS LIKE HAVING PART OF YOU WITH ME ALL THE TIME.

HEH...REMEMBER HOW ON NIGHTS LIKE THIS WE'D ALL COME UP TO THE ROOF TO SLEEP, BUT YOU'D STAY DOWN IN BED UNDER BLANKETS? YOU MUST HAVE SWELTERED.

ACHILLES? ARE YOU AWAKE?

OOO...

IT'S TOO *HOT*, DEIDAMIA.

IT'S *ALWAYS* TOO HOT--OR YOU'RE TOO *TIRED*. I DON'T KNOW *WHY* YOU'RE SO TIRED. ALL YOU DO IS GO HUNTING ALL DAY WITH PATROKLUS WHILE *I* HAVE TO MILK THE GOATS OR SPIN WOOL OR MAKE CHEESE.

YOU WERE NICER WHEN YOU WERE A *GIRL*.

WHAT'S WRONG? I'M SORRY--

WHAT HAVE I DONE WRONG?

NOTHING.

WHAT-- DO YOU SEE SOME-THING?

ACHILLES, IS SOMEONE THERE?

YES.

WHAT ARE YOU DOING OUT HERE?

IT'S TOO HOT TO SLEEP.

AND I'VE BEEN THINKING...

ABOUT WHAT?

WELL...ABOUT LEAVING SKYROS.

LEAVING! WHY?

YOU CAN'T GO!

ACHILLES, THE WAY LYKOMEDES LOOKS AT ME ... AND DEIDAMIA, SHE'S SO...

LOOK, YOU KNOW AS WELL AS I DO THAT NO ONE WANTS ME TO STAY.

I DO!

I...

WHAT?

I, UH...

WHAT?

ACHILLES...

I DON'T WANT YOU TO GO... NOT EVER...

ACHILLES, COME WITH ME.

YES, YES! I'LL LEAVE SKYROS WITH YOU...

NO--I MEAN *YES!* I MEAN *NOW*-- COME WITH ME DOWN THE HILL-- I KNOW A PLACE WE CAN BE ALONE TOGETHER.

ACHILLES...*SON*-- WHAT'S GOING ON?

LYKOMEDES.

I'M LEAVING SKYROS. I'M GOING TO MY FATHER PELEUS'S HOUSE IN PHTHIA.

I'M NOT COMING BACK.

OH? HAS HIGH KING AGAMEMNON ISSUED ANOTHER SUMMONS TO ASSAULT TROY?

OR IS IT SOMETHING-- OR SOME*ONE* --ELSE?

...SUCH AS... PATROKLUS?

IT'S PATROKLUS ...PARTLY...

BUT IT'S THE WAR, *TOO.* THERE'S NO SUMMONS YET -- BUT IT'LL COME. IT'S *HONOR* AND *STRENGTH* AND GLORY--

AND A NOT-SO-FAR-OFF *DEATH* IF I UNDERSTAND THE PRICE OF YOUR GLORY!

BETTER A GLORIOUS DEATH THAN TO BE TRAPPED FOR LIFE ON THIS ROCK OF DRY OBSCURITY! THIS IS *WORSE* THAN DEATH!

I SEE. OF COURSE. YOU'RE A CHILD OF THE *MAINLAND*...YOU'RE *YOUNG* LIKE IT-- AND *STUPID* LIKE IT. EVERYONE FORGETS THAT LONG AGO THE *ISLANDS* WERE BRIGHT JEWELS, MASTERS OF THE SEA AND LAND.

NOW THE MAINLAND RULES AND GROWS BRIGHT, OUTSHINING THE WISDOM OF THE ISLANDS. *OF COURSE* YOU LONG TO SHINE IN THE RAGING FIRE AND HEAT OF MAINLAND POWER, BURNING TOWARD THE BLINDING FLASH OF WAR. *OF COURSE.*

SO GO, YOU LOVER OF MEN AND WAR. GO AND BURN BRIGHT IN THE MOLTEN HEART OF BATTLE. SHED THE LIFE'S BLOOD OF ALL YOU *TRULY* LOVE.

CLUTCH FAST THE GLORY WHILE YOU CAN -- BEFORE IT'S DRAINED BY MAINLAND SPEARS AND BLED AWAY-- BEFORE YOU GLORIOUS WARRIORS BURN YOURSELVES OUT AND YOUR MAINLAND FALLS INTO ITS OWN DECLINE.

OF COURSE, NEOPTOLEMUS STAYS HERE.

NO, HE'S MY SON!

NOT ANY LONGER, YOU ARROGANT MAINLAND SCUM! HE'S A SON OF THE ISLANDS! YOU TURNED YOUR BACK ON MY DAUGHTER -- *GOOD!* I'M *GLAD* TO SEE YOU GO! BUT YOU WON'T TAKE MY GRANDSON WITH YOU!

HE'S MY SON!

DO YOU KNOW WHAT MEN SAY ABOUT ME? HOW I PUSHED THE GREAT THESEUS OVER THIS CLIFF? HOW'D *THAT* BE FOR A "GLORIOUS DEATH"?

THAT'S -- THAT'S NOT TRUE ABOUT THESEUS-- MALICIOUS GOSSIP! YOU WOULDN'T--

ARE YOU SURE? JUST TELL ME WHERE NEOPTOLEMUS WILL STAY.

KILLEEZ...

PYRRHUS... PYRRHUS... *YOU'LL* NEVER LEAVE ME, PYRRHUS. NEVER... NEVER... NEVER...

...IF I LEAVE FOR ITHAKA NOW...

...I CAN BE BACK LONG BEFORE WINTER BEGINS.

DON'T GO YET, ODYSSEUS. THERE ARE STILL SO MANY PLANS TO MAKE.

--AS LONG AS THE TROJANS HOLD HELEN, THEY HOLD OUR GRANDMOTHER, AITHRA, AS WELL. HOW MUCH LONGER MUST WE WAIT?

THE ARMY WILL NEED TIME TO REASSEMBLE, DEMOPHOON. AND I WON'T SUMMON THE ARMY TILL AFTER FIRST PLOWING. GO BACK TO EUBOEA--BOTH YOU AND AKAMAS--AND BE PATIENT.

POLYPOETES, SON OF PEIRITHOUS, IS AT THE GATE. HE WANTS TO KNOW WHEN--

YES, I KNOW. ONE OF HELEN'S WOMEN IS HIS AUNT. TELL HIM *AGAIN*, TALTHYBIUS, NOT BEFORE SPRING.

I CAN'T LET YOU GO HOME *YET*, ODYSSEUS. I NEED YOUR HELP COAXING PATIENCE FROM THESE KINGS... AND WE HAVEN'T DEALT WITH PALAMEDES YET.

SPARTA.

EUMENES'S FIELD YIELDED EIGHTY MEASURES OF GRAIN...

PRETEND AT LEAST, MENELAUS.

UH? GO ON...

POLIWOS'S FIELD YIELDED EIGHTY MEASURES OF GRAIN...

KUSAMENOS'S FIELD YIELDED NINETY-FIVE MEASURES OF GRAIN...

≥NGK≤

GUNOWAXEUS'S FIELD YIELDED...

GRANDFATHER! YOU STARTLED ME!

DIDN'T AWARD HIM MY DAUGHTER SO THAT HE'D *FAIL* HER. ≥NGK≤ OR THE THRONE OF LAKEDAEMON SO THAT HE'D FAIL *IT*...

MYCENAE.

WORD IS THAT THE TROJANS HAVE SUMMONED THEIR ALLIES -- MEN FROM PHRYGIA AND THRACE, KARIANS, PAEONIANS -- I DON'T REMEMBER THEM ALL AT THE MOMENT. IF WE WAIT MUCH LONGER, WE'LL BE OUTNUMBERED.

IT'S THE DEAD OF WINTER, DIOMEDES.

IF THE TROJANS CAN GATHER NOW, SO CAN THE ACHAEANS. WE BETTER STRIKE *THEM* BEFORE THEY ATTACK *US*!

BY THE TIME ALL THE ACHAEANS RECIEVE YOUR SUMMONS, WINTER WILL BE LONG OVER.

YES, IT'S TIME.

DIOMEDES, ODYSSEUS, I'M SENDING YOU TO SUMMON THE ACHAEANS TO AULIS AGAIN.

YES, HIGH KING.

WAIT! I HAVEN'T BEEN HOME TO ITHAKA YET--

ODYSSEUS, MY FRIEND, THIS IS A DELICATE MATTER. SOME OF THESE KINGS MAY NOT WANT TO JOIN A SECOND EXPEDITION AFTER THE FIRST ENDED SO DISMALLY. I NEED SOMEONE *PERSUASIVE* -- AND DIOMEDES? HE'S A GREAT FIGHTER, BUT--

YOU CAN VISIT YOUR ISLAND *AFTER* THE KINGS ARE SUMMONED TO AULIS. THERE WILL BE PLENTY OF TIME--MONTHS AND MONTHS--BEFORE THE FLEET'S READY TO SAIL FOR TROY.

NOW, QUICK! FOOD AND WINE FOR OUR GUEST! HE'S HAD A FROSTY RIDE FROM ARGOS! AND SOON HE'S OFF TO SPARTA, THEN PYLOS!

SPARTA.

ODYSSEUS OF ITHAKA AND DIOMEDES OF ARGOS.

MENELAUS, SON OF ATREUS! WE'VE BROUGHT YOU SUMMONS FROM AGAMEMNON!

SUMMONS?

TO AULIS! BRING YOUR SHIPS AND MEN! WE'RE OFF TO ATTACK TROY!

PRAISE THE GODS! AT LAST!

NESTOR OF PYLOS.

OF COURSE I'LL JOIN THE ARMY AGAIN. BUT I SUSPECT THAT MANY OF THE ACHAEANS WON'T BE SO WILLING. AGAMEMNON'S TIMING IS FAR FROM CONVENIENT. THE HARVEST WAS LATE AND LEAN... WINTER'S BEEN HARD...

LET ME COME WITH YOU TO THE OTHER KINGS.

IF ANY KING PROVES A RELUCTANT WARRIOR, I'LL GLADLY RECOUNT A TALE TO REMIND HIM HOW EAGERLY HIS FATHER HEEDED ANY CALL TO ARMS.

AGAPENOR OF ARKADIA.

I'M SURPRISED THE HIGH KING SUMMONS ME AGAIN, LANDLOCKED AND SHIPLESS AS I AM. AGAMEMNON LENT US SHIPS THE FIRST TIME... AND WE LOST SO MANY OF THEM IN THAT STORM...

PALAMEDES OF NAUPLIA.

I GRIEVE FOR MY MEN. THEY SPENT TWO YEARS THE FIRST TIME, WAITING TO CONQUER TROY, ONLY TO MEET FRUSTRATION. AND JUST AS THEY'VE SETTLED BACK INTO THEIR NEGLECTED LIVES, WITH A THIN HARVEST, A BITTER WINTER, AND BAD FISHING, THEY'VE GOT TO START ALL OVER AGAIN...

GREAT AJAX OF SALAMIS.

BACK TO TROY?

HMF.

I HOPE AGAMEMNON KNOWS HIS WAY THIS TIME...

MENESTHEUS OF ATHENS.

I'VE GOT A CITY TO RULE. GO ASK THE SONS OF THESEUS--YOU KNOW, AKAMAS AND DEMOPHOON. THEY'LL BE WETTING THEMSELVES IN ANTICIPATION.

PENELEOS OF BOEOTIA.

LAST TIME, THE GREAT HERO THERSANDER, SON OF POLYNEIKES, FELL IN A BATTLE THAT WAS ALL FOR NOTHING. TELL ME, HOW WILL THIS TIME BE ANY DIFFERENT?

ASKALAPHUS OF ORCHOMENOS.

WHAT? MORE RUSHING OFF TO WHO-KNOWS-WHERE? FIGHTING NOBODY-KNOWS-WHO? LOSING NO-ONE-KNOWS-HOW-MANY SHIPS AND MEN? AREN'T WE ALL GETTING A BIT OLD FOR THIS?

OF THE KINGS WE'VE REACHED IN THESE PAST FEW MONTHS, ELEVEN ARE EAGERLY PREPARING THEIR FLEETS TO SAIL TO AULIS. MOST OF THE RELUCTANT ONES --INCLUDING THOSE WHO'VE COME TO MYCENAE TO CONSULT YOU IN PERSON--WILL BE SWAYED TO JOIN AS SOON AS YOU GO TO AULIS. THEY JUST NEED TO SEE *YOUR* COMMITMENT...

...BUT SOME OF THEM JUST WON'T LISTEN-- NO MATTER HOW LONG NESTOR BLATHERS ON ABOUT THEIR FORE- FATHERS' GLORIOUS BATTLES.

THERE'S STILL THE SUITORS' VOW. THEY CAN'T ESCAPE THAT.

MOST OF THEM CONSIDER THAT FULFILLED THE FIRST TIME. KINYRAS OF CYPRUS'S LITTLE DISPLAY OF TOY BOATS CERTAINLY DIDN'T HELP. YOU SHOULDN'T HAVE LET HIM GET AWAY WITH THAT.

HE DIDN'T. HE'S DEAD.

WHAT?

KINYRAS FAILED HIS VOW-- NOW HE'S *DEAD. THAT'S* HOW THE GODS REWARD THE FAITHLESS. TELL *THAT* TO THE ACHAEAN KINGS.

I'LL SAIL FOR AULIS AS SOON AS POSSIBLE. WE'LL SEE WHO DARES TO REMAIN BEHIND.

MAYBE I SHOULD HAVE *PALAMEDES* SUMMON THE SHIRKERS. HE SEEMS TO BE MORE CLEVER THAN YOU AT THAT SORT OF THING.

AGAME-MNON, LISTEN TO ME.

YOU CAN FORCE THE KINGS OF THE ACHAEANS TO GO TO TROY--YOU'RE THE HIGH KING, COMMANDER OF THE ARMY, YOU CAN INVOKE THE GODS AND LEVY FINES. BUT IF OUR FIGHTING MEN DON'T BELIEVE IN THIS CAUSE, YOU'VE LOST ALREADY.

CAREFUL WHAT YOU SAY TO ME, ODYSSEUS.

YOU NEED TO FIND SOMETHING FOR THE MEN TO RALLY AROUND --FOR THEM TO BELIEVE IN... NOT TRADE ROUTES OR TAXES OR RANK AMONG KINGS, BUT SOMETHING THEY CAN SEE AND TOUCH.

THEY BELIEVE IN THE GLORY OF WAR--RICHES WHEN WE TRIUMPH, HONOR IF WE FALL IN BATTLE!

DOESN'T MEAN MUCH TO SOMEONE COLD AND HUNGRY.

THEN THEY'LL FIGHT FOR THEIR WOMEN AND CHILDREN. NO ACHAEAN HOUSEHOLD IS SAFE IF WE LET THE TROJANS GET AWAY WITH PLUNDERING MENELAUS.

YES, THAT'S BETTER. DO YOU REMEMBER WHAT TYNDAREUS TOLD THE ACHAEANS WHEN HE WANTED A HUSBAND FOR HELEN?

HE SAID SHE WAS THE MOST BEAUTIFUL WOMAN IN THE WORLD. AND SHE IS BEAUTIFUL, BUT I'M NOT SURE SHE'S THE MOST--

IT DOESN'T MATTER! MOST OF THE ARMY HAS NEVER SEEN HER, BUT EVERYONE KNOWS HELEN HAD FORTY-ONE OF THE HIGHEST-BORN ACHAEANS COMPETING TO MARRY HER-- MORE NOBLE SUITORS THAN ANYONE EVER HEARD OF BEFORE.

HOW COULD SHE NOT BE THE MOST BEAUTIFUL WOMAN IN THE WORLD?

SHE ALREADY HAS THE REPUTATION --LET'S USE IT!

PROMISE THE MEN HELEN, THE MOST BEAUTIFUL WOMAN IN THE WORLD. PROMISE THEM HER SMILE, THE SCENT OF HER HAIR AND HER BREASTS, MAYBE EVEN A GRATEFUL CARESS --AND THEY'LL TEAR TROY APART STONE BY STONE WITH THEIR FINGERNAILS TO REACH HER. *HELEN'S* WHAT WILL MAKE TROY FALL.

I ADMIT IT, ODYSSEUS. YOU'RE CLEVER. YOU'RE *BRILLIANT*.

AND IF *THAT* PLAN DOESN'T WORK, I'M SURE YOU'LL THINK UP ANOTHER THAT'S EVEN BETTER.

OH, IT'LL WORK--EVEN ON THE ONES WHOSE PASSION IS FOR MEN.

AND *I'M* LEAVING FOR ITHAKA IN THE MORNING.

HA HA! HOW CAN I LET SUCH A CLEVER MAN GO? BUT I SUPPOSE--

HIGH KING...

KALCHAS? WHAT'S THIS?

≡HEM≡ HIGH KING, I COME TO YOU NOT AS THE VOICE OF THE GOD, BUT AS ≡HEM≡ ONE *FATHER* TO ANOTHER, A FATHER WHO SEES HOW GREATLY YOU LOVE YOUR OWN DAUGHTERS.

MY CHILDREN ARE MY MOST PRECIOUS POSSESSIONS. COME HERE, IPHIGENIA, ELEKTRA, CHRYSOTHEMIS...

≈HEM≈...I HAVE A DAUGHTER, TOO... MY CRESSIDA--SHE'S STILL IN TROY ≈HEM≈...

HIGH KING, THINK FOR A MOMENT HOW YOU'D FEEL IF MYCENAE WERE ATTACKED, IF YOUR DAUGHTERS WERE THREATENED--

THREATENED! WHAT DO YOU MEAN?

HIGH KING, PLEASE --CRESSIDA IS AS PRECIOUS TO ME--≈HEM≈

HOW DARE YOU PLAY ON MY LOVE FOR MY DAUGHTERS! YOU'VE GIVEN US NOTHING BUT DELAYS AND DEMANDS AND NOT A WORD WHEN WE MISSED TROY IN THE FOG!

PLEASE, HIGH KING, DON'T PUNISH MY DAUGHTER FOR MY FAILINGS--

HOW DARE YOU USE MY DAUGHTERS-- HOW DID YOU GET THEM TO--?

KLYTEMNESTRA! YOU'RE BEHIND THIS--USING MY CHILDREN AGAINST ME--

NO! KALCHAS IS ASKING YOU TO SAVE HIS DAUGHTER! HE SAID YOU WOULDN'T LISTEN BEFORE. I THOUGHT YOUR OWN DAUGHTERS MIGHT SOFTEN YOUR HEART.

BUT I SHOULD HAVE KNOWN BETTER! HOW COULD I FORGET THE WAY YOU TREAT OTHER PEOPLE'S CHILDREN?

LIAR! YOU'RE ALL LIARS! ALL YOU ACHAEANS! I WAS SUCH A FOOL!

YOU SAID IT WAS ALL A MISTAKE-- AND I BELIEVED YOU! I WELCOMED YOU!

ATTACK TROY! PAH! YOU NEVER WENT TO TROY!

AND THE WOUND!

IT--IT CAN'T BE...

THE GREATEST HEALERS IN THE WORLD, YOU SAID! MORE LIES! LIE AFTER LIE!

IT'S THE WOUND THAT NEVER HEALS! AN ENDLESS PAIN TO DRIVE ME MAD!

WHY? WHY? WHY DIDN'T YOU JUST KILL ME?

...TELEPHUS!

QUICK! CARRY HIM OUTSIDE THE WALLS!

AGAMEMNON, JUST A MOMENT! HE'S KING OF TEUTHRANIA-- THIS IS YOUR CHANCE TO MAKE THE MYSIANS OUR ALLIES AND KEEP THEM FROM JOINING THE TROJANS.

WAIT! CARRY HIM INTO THE GREAT HALL! A WARM HEARTH WILL DO HIM GOOD.

SURE YOU WANT HIM OUT OF THE OPEN AIR?

WATCH HIS WOUND!

WHAT A STINK!

TLEPOLEMUS, DO YOU KNOW WHAT HE WAS RAVING ABOUT?

HE'S JUST MAD!

PERHAPS...BUT MAYBE, MAYBE SOMETHING'S HAPPENED THAT'S PREYING ON HIS MIND.

THERE'S BEEN MADNESS IN HIS FAMILY BEFORE... REMEMBER HERAKLES?

I KNOW THE STORY WELL --HOW HERAKLES WENT MAD AND IN HIS BLINDNESS SLEW HIS CHILDREN.

SLEW HIS--?

IPHIGENIA! ELEKTRA! CHRYSOTHEMIS! STAY BACK!

SET HIM THERE. THAT'S GOOD. AND STIR UP THE FIRE-- IT'LL HELP WITH THE STINK.

ELEKTRA! COME BACK!

NO! I WANNA SEE!

I'LL GET HER!

uhhh...

KILISSA, NO! DON'T TAKE ORESTES ANY CLOSER!

ELEKTRA!

GIVE ORESTES TO ME!

OH!

EW! HE'S STINKY!

TAKE MY CHILDREN OUT OF HERE --NOW!

LOOK!

CAREFUL!

WHAT'S HE--?

LEMME GO, KILISSA!

OH, PRAISE THE MOTHER--

AAAH!

AAAAH!

AAAAH!

BRING ACHILLES TO ME OR I'LL RIP THIS CHILD APART!

--AAAAA--

YOU REEKING PIECE OF FILTH! COME DOWN FROM THERE!

OH-H-H-H!

THE GOD... THE GOD SPEAKS!

THE ACHAEANS WILL NEVER TAKE TROY WITHOUT THE HELP OF TELEPHUS, KING OF TEUTHRANIA! NOT WITHOUT THE HELP OF TELEPHUS, KING OF TEUTHRANIA! UHHHH...

KALCHAS?

AGAMEMNON?

=HEM=

ANOTHER PROPHECY BY A TROJAN PRIEST --ABOUT A TROJAN ALLY--HOW CONVENIENT!

AGAMEMNON, BE CAREFUL! THAT PROPHECY WAS FROM THE GOD!

AGAMEMNON, HOW ABOUT THIS? OFFER TO BRING ACHILLES TO TELEPHUS IF TELEPHUS SWEARS TO JOIN US AGAINST TROY.

YES! THE GODS WILL BE SATISFIED, AND YOUR SON WILL BE SAFE!

HMMM.

MAKE THE OFFER.

TELEPHUS, AGREE TO JOIN US AGAINST TROY AND AGAMEMNON WILL IMMEDIATELY SUMMON ACHILLES FROM HIS FATHER'S HOUSE IN PHTHIA.

NO! I'LL NEVER JOIN SUCH LIARS AND TORMENTERS AGAINST MY SON'S FAMILY!

YOU ALL HEARD HIM REFUSE! HE CAN'T STAY UP THERE FOREVER. WHEN HE STEPS DOWN, HE DIES!

NO! WE NEED HIM IN ORDER TO TAKE TROY!

ORESTES!

WAIT! TELEPHUS, WE WON'T ASK YOU TO FIGHT THE TROJANS. JUST PROMISE NOT TO AID THEM. AND YOU MUST SHOW US THE WAY TO TROY -- GUIDE OUR FLEET THERE.

FATHER, GUIDE ME...

I...

I'LL DO THAT MUCH. BRING ACHILLES TO HEAL ME AND I'LL DENY AID TO TROY...

...AND I'LL GUIDE YOU THERE... IF THAT'S WHERE YOU TRULY WISH TO GO.

I SWEAR UPON THIS ALTAR.

GOOD, GOOD, NOW WHY DON'T YOU STEP DOWN?

FIRST, ACHILLES! BRING ME ACHILLES!

AGAMEMNON?

I SWEAR TO SUMMON ACHILLES TO MEET US AT AULIS. I'LL SEND ODYSSEUS TO PHTHIA FOR HIM *TODAY.*

BUT I'M LEAVING FOR ITHAKA--

YOU'LL FETCH ACHILLES! YOU'RE *OBVIOUSLY* THE *ONLY* ONE CLEVER ENOUGH TO OUT-WIT HIM IF HE TRIES TO HIDE AGAIN.

TELEPHUS, THE HIGH KING HAS SWORN BEFORE US ALL TO BRING ACHILLES TO YOU. WHILE I AM KING OF PYLOS AND THE ELDEST HERE, HE WILL FULFILL HIS VOW AND YOU WON'T BE HARMED. NOW, PLEASE, COME DOWN ... AND GIVE ME THE CHILD.

ODYSSEUS--*AND* NESTOR --WILL DEPART FOR PHTHIA *IMMEDIATELY.* THE REST OF US SAIL FOR AULIS TOMORROW... AND FROM THERE, TELEPHUS GUIDES US TO TROY.

PHTHIA.

GREAT SPERCHEUS, WHOSE WATERS SHED LIFE ON PHTHIA, I VOW THAT WHEN MY SON RETURNS FROM THE WAR AT TROY, HE'LL CUT OFF HIS HAIR FOR YOU AND SACRIFICE FIFTY YOUNG RAMS TO YOUR SPRINGS.

SPERCHEUS, I DEDICATE MY HAIR TO YOU.

WHILE I KEEP ALL BLADES FROM MY HAIR, TURN ALL BLADES FROM ME, SO THAT MY SHORT LIFE WILL STRETCH LONG ENOUGH TO LET ME TOUCH YOUR WATERS ONCE AGAIN.

ACCEPT THIS DEDICATION.

ACHILLES, MY SON, THESE MONTHS YOU'VE SPENT IN PHTHIA ARE PRECIOUS TO ME, BUT NOW I'M SENDING YOU TO WAR A SECOND TIME.

I GAVE YOU GIFTS THE FIRST TIME --MY SPEAR AND SHIELD, GIFTS TO ME FROM MORTALS --THE BEST I COULD GIVE...

I DIDN'T DARE TEMPT THE GODS' ANGER BY PASSING ON WHAT THEY GAVE ME THE DAY I WED YOUR MOTHER. BUT NOW MY PRIDE IN YOU DEMANDS IT. I GIVE YOU IMMORTAL GIFTS --THE BEST I HAVE.

THESE ARE XANTHUS AND BALIUS, CHILDREN OF PODARGE, A MARE BRED BY THE IMMORTALS. HARNESS THEM TO YOUR WAR CHARIOT--THEY'LL NEVER FAIL YOU.

AND MY ARMOR...IT'S YOURS NOW. IMMORTAL ARMOR. WHILE I WORE IT, NO MAN COULD CUT ME DOWN. MAY THE GODS GRANT THE SAME TO YOU, MY SON.

THANK YOU, FATHER. WHEN I RIDE INTO BATTLE, MY FOES WILL TREMBLE, KNOWING THEY FACE THE SON OF THE HERO PELEUS SON OF AEAKUS SON OF ZEUS.

THE TALES I COULD TELL OF YOUR FOREFATHERS, SON OF PELEUS, IF ONLY TIME PERMITTED...

YES, YOU'VE FEASTED US IN YOUR FATHER'S HOUSE AND MADE THE PROPER OFFERINGS TO THE GODS. NOW THE HIGH KING IS WAITING AT AULIS--

LET HIM WAIT! I'M NOT A BEAST YOKED BY AGAMEMNON OR BOUND BY ANY OATH TO AVENGE HIS BROTHER! I'M JOINING HIS ARMY BECAUSE I CHOOSE TO.

ACHILLES, NO ONE SAYS YOU--

TELEPHUS HAS MORE CLAIM ON ME THAN AGAMEMNON--

ACHILLES! OUR DESTINIES ARE IN THE GODS' HANDS. BUT WE CAN MASTER OURSELVES. KEEP YOUR TEMPER.

HOLD THAT FIRE WITHIN YOUR CHEST UNTIL YOU MEET A FOE. STRIFE AMONG COMRADES IS DISASTROUS. CHOOSE FRIENDSHIP, AND THE ACHAEANS YOUNG AND OLD WILL READILY HONOR YOU.

SEE? YOUR STAUNCHEST FRIENDS SURROUND YOU-- PHOENIX, SON OF AMYNTOR, WHO DID MORE TO REAR YOU THAN I EVER DID...

MENESTHIUS, SON OF BORUS AND YOUR SISTER, POLYDORA...

THE GREAT WARRIORS EUDORUS, SON OF THE GOD, AND PISANDER, MAEMALUS'S SON...

YOUR LOYAL COMPANIONS, AUTOMEDON, SON OF DIORES, AND ALKIMUS, SON OF LAERKES...

...AND THE MAN YOU RANK BEFORE ALL OTHERS--PATROKLUS, SON OF MY OLD FRIEND MENOETIUS OF OPOIS, WHO BIDS HIS OWN SON FAREWELL TODAY.

MY SON, STRIVE TO BE THE GREATEST WARRIOR. BUT BE A GREAT LEADER, TOO. DON'T FORGET THAT ANY VOYAGE WILL FAIL IF THE ROWERS DON'T PULL TOGETHER.

I UNDERSTAND, FATHER.

PATROKLUS, DON'T FORGET WHAT I TOLD YOU WHEN THESE ROYAL GUESTS ARRIVED WITH THEIR SUMMONS. GUIDE ACHILLES, GIVE HIM SOUND COUNSEL. HE MAY BE OF NOBLER BIRTH, BUT YOU'RE OLDER. HE LISTENS TO YOU, IT'S OBVIOUS. *REMEMBER.*

FATHER, I WILL. I VALUE HIS LIFE AS MUCH AS I VALUE MY OWN.

SON OF AEAKUS! MORE VISITORS!

WE'LL BE BACK TO THE HOUSE SHORTLY. MAKE THEM WELCOME.

WE TRIED, BUT THEY WOULDN'T STAY AT THE HOUSE. SHE INSISTED ON COMING HERE IMMEDIATELY.

SHE? WHO?

THETIS.

THETIS?

MOTHER?

ACHILLES? IS THAT YOU?

MOTHER!

HERE THEY COME.

ACHILLES!

THANK THE GODS I'M NOT TOO LATE! I WAS AFRAID YOU'D HAVE LEFT FOR THE WAR ALREADY.

MOTHER! IT'S REALLY YOU! I CAN HARDLY BELIEVE YOU'RE HERE!

STEP UP BESIDE ME, ACHILLES, AND WE'LL GO.

NO, YOU COME DOWN. COME AND SPEAK TO FATHER.

I HAVE NOTHING TO SAY TO THAT MAN.

PLEASE, MOTHER, YOU AND FATHER ARE BOTH HERE. WHY WON'T YOU TAKE THIS OPPORTUNITY--

THE QUESTION ISN'T WHY SHE DOESN'T SPEAK TO ME, BUT WHY SHE'S HERE AT ALL, UNEXPECTED, UNANNOUNCED, INTERRUPTING OUR RITES--

INTERRUPTING *YOUR* RITES! HOW DARE YOU, WHEN *YOU'RE* THE FOOL WHO INTERRUPTED *MY* RITE TO FOREVER PRESERVE OUR SON FROM DANGER. THE *WORST* NIGHT OF MY *LIFE*--

BUT AT LEAST IT GAVE ME THE STRENGTH TO *LEAVE* YOU AT LAST! *I* WAS THE FOOL TO EVER *MARRY* YOU--

PLEASE, MOTHER, DON'T FIGHT WITH HIM. YOU'RE HIS *WIFE! ACT* LIKE IT.

SHE LEFT ME *LONG* AGO. SHE SHOULD HAVE STAYED AWAY.

FATHER, DON'T SAY THAT! YOUR WEDDING WAS BLESSED BY ALL THE GODS --IT'S *LEGENDARY!* CAN'T YOU--

LOOK HARD AT YOUR OWN MARRIAGE, ACHILLES, BEFORE YOU QUESTION MINE.

ACHILLES, MY PRECIOUS SON, I WAS BORN IN SERVICE TO THE GODS, RAISED BY THE GODDESS. I'D HOPED TO BE A BRIDE TO A GOD. BUT BECAUSE MY SON WAS DESTINED TO BE GREATER THAN HIS FATHER, THE GODDESS WED ME TO A MORTAL INSTEAD.

AND NOT EVEN THE GREATEST OF MORTALS -- A QUARRELSOME BROTHER-KILLER RULING A SECOND-RATE KINGDOM OF RABBLE AND REFUGEES. I WAS BITTERLY DISAPPOINTED. BUT I HAD ONE JOY FROM IT...

YOU.

THE FIRST TIME I LEFT PHTHIA, I LEFT YOU BEHIND. I WON'T MAKE THAT MISTAKE AGAIN. YOUR FATHER SENDS YOU TO A WAR THAT MEANS IMMINENT DEATH FOR YOU. BUT COME WITH ME AND I'LL KEEP YOU SAFE INTO OLD AGE.

THETIS, DON'T INTERFERE...

I **WARN** YOU, PELEUS--

OR WHAT? WHAT THREATS CAN YOU MAKE SO FAR FROM HOME, DAUGHTER OF OCEAN? WILL YOU RAISE THE SPERCHEUS RIVER AGAINST ME? AGAINST OUR SON?

ARE YOU BELITTLING MY POWER? YOU WERE PRETTY QUICK TO CRY FOR ME WHEN ROCKS THREATENED TO RIP THE ARGO'S HULL ON YOUR VOYAGE BACK FROM KOLCHIS. YOU DIDN'T MIND MY INTERFERENCE WHEN MY SISTERS AND I PRAYED THE WAVES TO WASH YOU SAFELY PAST.

STOP IT, BOTH OF YOU!

MOTHER, MY DECISION IS MADE. I MADE IT LONG AGO ON SKYROS WHERE YOU LEFT ME DISGUISED AS A GIRL, LEFT ME FOR YEARS WITHOUT ANY WORD...

YOU WERE **SAFE** THERE--

MY DECISION IS STILL THE SAME. I'M GOING TO AULIS TO JOIN THE ACHAEANS AGAINST TROY--

NO! NO! ACHILLES, LISTEN TO ME -- THAT WAR BRINGS YOU DEATH --

NOT ONLY DEATH, MOTHER. GLORY, TOO. EVERYONE DIES. BUT NOT EVERYONE ACHIEVES--

BUT NOT SO **SOON!**

MOTHER, I'M GOING TO TROY.

NO, ACHILLES, **NO!** I'VE **SEEN** IT--YOUR DEATH. YOU'LL KILL A CHILD OF THE SUN GOD, AND IN RETURN THE GOD WILL KILL **YOU!** I **WON'T** LET THAT HAPPEN!

I'M GOING, MOTHER.

ACHILLES...

THEN I'M GOING, TOO.

YOU? MY *MOTHER*? LIKE A CAMP FOLLOWER? THEY'LL ALL LAUGH!

LAUGH AT THETIS WHO KNOWS THE GODS? LET THEM LAUGH IF THEY DARE!

ODYSSEUS, MAYBE YOU SHOULDN'T...

THE DAUGHTER OF OCEAN IN A WAR CAMP? IT'S *UNHEARD* OF FOR A WOMAN OF *YOUR* DEGREE...

MY MOTHER GOES WHERE SHE *CHOOSES*, ODYSSEUS!

AND IF SHE WANTS TO FOLLOW ME TO TROY, THEN SHE WILL.

AULIS.

THOSE SHIPS ENTERING THE BAY--ARE THOSE ACHILLES'S?

YES. I BELIEVE SO.

GOOD. THAT MEANS ODYSSEUS AND NESTOR, TOO. I WANT THIS TELEPHUS BUSINESS FINISHED SO WE CAN GET ON WITH THIS EXPEDITION.

HOW SOON CAN WE BE READY TO SAIL FOR TROY?

MONTHS YET. WE'RE STILL WAITING FOR MORE SHIPS. RIGHT NOW WE'RE BARELY HALF THE STRENGTH OF LAST TIME.

WE'LL NEED *MORE* STRENGTH THAN LAST TIME IF RUMOR'S RIGHT AND THE TROJANS ARE CASTING FAR AND WIDE FOR ALLIES.

I THINK IT'S THE DEER, AGAMEMNON. NONE OF THEM IS GETTING FOOD HALF SO--

WHAT DO THEY EXPECT? THEY GET *PLENTY* OF GRAIN, OIL, AND WINE FROM DELOS. I CAN'T SHARE ONE DEER AMONG HUNDREDS OF MEN. IF THEY WANT VENISON, THEY SHOULD *HUNT!*

THEIR EQUIPMENT ISN'T AS GOOD AS OURS. AND CERTAINLY YOU REALIZE, WITH THE WAR COMING, THEY CAN'T WASTE ARROWS.

SINCE YOU KNOW SO MUCH ABOUT THE MEN, PALAMEDES, *YOU* TAKE CARE OF THEM! I WON'T DISCUSS IT HERE.

HE JUST SHOT A DEER--WHY IS *HE* IN A BAD MOOD?

YOU NEVER KNOW WHEN TO STOP, DO YOU, PALAMEDES?

WHAT?

...uhhhh...

...uhhhh...

I DON'T UNDERSTAND. THE WOUND WAS *HEALING* WHEN WE LEFT MYSIA. BUT THAT-- THAT'S *WORSE* THAN BEFORE. I CAN'T HEAL *THAT.*

HE WON'T LET ANYONE ELSE TOUCH HIM. ONLY YOU, ACHILLES.

HE CLAIMS THE SUN GOD'S ORACLE AT PATARA IN LYKIA TOLD HIM "THE WOUNDER MUST HEAL." YOU *ARE* THE ONE WHO WOUNDED HIM, AREN'T YOU?

YES, OF COURSE, I PLUNGED MY SPEAR RIGHT INTO HIS LEFT THIGH. BUT THAT ROTTING MESS IS BEYOND MY ABILITIES.

SOMEONE BETTER HELP HIM *SOON* OR ELSE HE'LL--WELL... WHAT ABOUT MACHAON AND PODALIRIUS?

STILL IN TRIKKA, BUT IT DOESN'T MATTER. HE'D NEVER LET THEM NEAR. HE THINKS *THEY* MADE THE WOUND WORSE, NOT BETTER.

HE'S THE ONE WHO MADE IT WORSE, SCRATCHING AND TEARING AT IT AND SPOUTING MADNESS. BUT KALCHAS SAYS WE NEED HIM TO WIN THE WAR, SO DO WHAT YOU CAN, ACHILLES.

"THE WOUNDER MUST HEAL..."

"THE *WOUNDER...*"

THE SPEAR! IT'S ACHILLES'S *SPEAR!* THE SUN GOD'S ORACLE SAID, "THE *WOUNDER* MUST HEAL." THE SPEAR IS THE *ACTUAL* WOUNDER.

ARE *YOU* MAD, TOO, ODYSSEUS? HOW CAN A SPEAR HEAL *ANYTHING?*

THERE'S PRECEDENT--MY COUSIN MELAMPUS CURED IPHIKLUS'S IMPOTENCE USING THE KNIFE THAT CAUSED IT. OF COURSE, THAT WAS MORE A WOUND OF THE MIND THAN THE FLESH.

IS THIS ANY *DIFFERENT?* TELEPHUS WOULDN'T TEAR AT HIS WOUND IF HE WEREN'T *MAD.*

KALCHAS, YOU'RE A PRIEST OF THE SUN GOD. WILL ACHILLES'S SPEAR HEAL TELEPHUS?

OH! UH--≥HEM≤ IF THE ORACLE SAID SO, IT MUST BE TRUE... ≥HEM≤

FINE. I'LL FETCH MY SPEAR, BUT I WANT *YOU* TO FETCH MACHAON AND PODALIRIUS FROM TRIKKA. TELEPHUS MAY NOT WANT THEIR HELP, BUT *I* WANT IT. AND THE *ARMY* WILL NEED THEM AT TROY.

...uhh...

TELEPHUS?

MANY DAYS LATER.

DAYS LATER STILL.

...STILL SEE THAT EVIL GRIN ON MACHAON'S FACE THE DAY YOUR FLEET LEFT MYSIA -- IT LINGERS, HIS PRETENSE OF CONCERN WHILE SECRETLY MOCKING ME, PROLONGING MY WOUND WHILE PRETENDING TO HEAL--

BUT THE WOUND *WAS* HEALING THAT DAY. MACHAON TREATED IT PROPERLY. I *STILL* DON'T UNDERSTAND HOW IT GOT WORSE.

WHAT?

...UH--

CURSE IT, YOU'RE RIGHT. I DON'T KNOW... I DON'T KNOW WHAT TO TRUST ANYMORE. SOMEHOW-- SOMETHING STILL SEEMS WRONG. I CAN'T EVEN TRUST *MYSELF*.

YOU'RE THE ONLY ONE I TRUST, ACHILLES. YOU'VE TREATED ME WITH RESPECT. PROMISE ME -- AFTER WE REACH TROY -- TAKE ME BACK TO TEUTHRANIA. I FEAR I'LL NEVER MAKE IT ON MY OWN.

I PROMISE, TELEPHUS. I'LL GET YOU HOME SAFELY. YOU'RE A LOT BETTER NOW, YOUR LEG'S HEALING. JUST KEEP YOUR STRENGTH UP. GIVE THE WOUND PLENTY OF FRESH AIR, AND PUT YARROW POULTICES ON IT AT NIGHT THE WAY I'VE SHOWN YOU.

AND WHEN I GET THERE, OEDIPUS'S GRAVE WILL BE WAITING ON HIGH TO GREET ME. THAT PART WAS REAL, WASN'T IT? YES.

IT'S NOT--

NO, *NO*! NOT OEDIPUS -- HIS *GRANDSON*.

MY MIND'S SO CLOUDY STILL...

...SO THEN HE TELLS THIS STORY THAT I DON'T THINK EVEN NESTOR KNOWS ...HOW YEARS AGO HE LEFT TEGEA IN SEARCH OF HIS MOTHER AND ENDED UP IN TEUTHRANIA WHERE HE KILLED AN OUTLAW WHO'D BEEN TERRORIZING THE PEOPLE THERE.

THE KING, TEUTHRAS, WAS SO GRATEFUL HE MADE TELEPHUS HIS HEIR AND GAVE HIS ADOPTED DAUGHTER TO TELEPHUS IN MARRIAGE. ONLY THE DAUGHTER WAS ACTUALLY TELEPHUS'S MOTHER.

HA! *WHAT?*

HE HADN'T SEEN HER SINCE HE WAS A CHILD, SO THEY DIDN'T RECOGNIZE EACH OTHER UNTIL THEY WERE ABOUT TO HAVE SEX. WHEN SHE MENTIONED HERAKLES, HE REALIZED WHO SHE WAS JUST IN TIME TO AVOID INCEST.

YOU BELIEVE THIS STORY?

DOESN'T MATTER WHETHER *I* BELIEVE IT. *HE* DOES. HE'S INCREDIBLY SENSITIVE ABOUT IT. THAT'S WHY THERSANDER'S GRAVE DROVE HIM CRAZY. HE THOUGHT THAT OUR BURYING A GRANDSON OF INCEST SO PROMINENTLY WAS DELIBERATE MOCKERY.

THAT'S WHAT MADE HIM RE-OPEN THE WOUND AND WANDER ALL OVER THE PLACE, RAGGED AND FILTHY, LIKE SOME ADDLED BEGGAR?

IT DOESN'T SEEM LIKE ENOUGH, DOES IT? MAYBE THERE'S MORE. MAYBE WE'LL NEVER KNOW.

WELL, I'M JUST GLAD YOU'RE NOT SPENDING YOUR NIGHTS WITH *HIM* ANYMORE.

SHSHSHSHSHSHSHSH

SHSHSHSHSHSHSHSHSHSHSHSH

SON OF NELEUS!

SHSHSHSHSHSHSHSHSHSHSHSHSHSHSHSHSHSHSH SHSHSHSHSHSHSHSHSHSH

NESTOR, I NEED TO TALK TO YOU ...NEED YOUR ADVICE...

I SEE...COME, LET'S WALK.

SHSHSHSHSHSHSHSHSHSHSHSHSHSHSHSHSHSHSHSHSHSHSHSHSHSHSHSHSHSHSHSHSHSHSH

RIGHT NOW WE'RE ONLY DOING THE LEEWARD SIDES. OTHERWISE THE WIND BLOWS DIRT INTO THE PITCH.

IF THIS WIND WOULD JUST STOP...

IT'LL STOP WHEN...

...WHEN MY DAUGHTER DIES AT THE ALTAR.

THEN IT'S TRUE, THE RUMOR THAT'S BURNING THROUGH THE CAMP. ARTEMIS DEMANDS YOUR DAUGHTER IN ORDER FOR THE FLEET TO SAIL.

BUT I CAN'T-- IF I COULD GET AWAY--

SHSHSHSHSHSHSHSHSHSHSHSHSHSHSHSHSHSHSHSHSHSHSHSHSHSHSHSHSHSHSHSHSHSHSHSH

LEAVE
ME
ALONE!

YES...

...FOR TROY TO FALL, THE FIRST-BORN DAUGHTER OF AGAMEMNON MUST DIE.

I'M BOUND BY HONOR TO RESCUE HER IF SHE ASKS ME TO, MOTHER.

IF YOU RESCUE HER, YOU WON'T SAIL FOR TROY. THAT'S WHAT I'VE WANTED ALL ALONG... BUT NOW-- I FEAR A BATTLE AT THE ALTAR.

MOTHER, DEATH LIES IN WAIT FOR EVERYONE.

YOUR DEATH WILL COME FROM THE SUN GOD IN RETRIBUTION FOR YOUR SLAYING A SON OF HIS.

I HAVEN'T SLAIN ONE YET.

I CAN MAKE SURE YOU NEVER DO.

MNEMON, COME HERE.

MNEMON CAN RECOGNIZE THE SUN GOD'S CHILDREN. FROM NOW ON HE'LL ACCOMPANY YOU INTO BATTLE TO STEER YOU AWAY FROM EVERY SON OF THE GOD.

CAN YOU FIGHT, MNEMON?

I'LL FIGHT WELL FOR YOU, SON OF THE NEREID, AND KEEP YOU SAFE.

VERY GOOD ANSWER.

THEN PUT ON ARMOR AND GET READY FOR BATTLE.

BUT WE WON'T FACE THE SUN GOD TONIGHT. THE GIRL IS CLAIMED BY ARTEMIS OF THE HUNT, THE MOON GODDESS.

TAKE MY BLESSING WITH YOU, ALL OF YOU...

THANK YOU, MOTHER.

LET'S GO!

...AND REMEMBER THAT THE SUN GOD ALWAYS FOLLOWS HIS SISTER, THE MOON.

IS THE GAG NECESSARY?

IF SHE COULD SPEAK, SHE MIGHT CURSE US.

CURSE US? NOT IPHIGENIA.

I REMEMBER HOW SHE SANG FOR US ONCE WHEN I WAS A GUEST AT MYCENAE...

...A VOICE THE GODS MIGHT ENVY.

IT'S RAINING-- YOU'LL BE ILL...

EVEN THE SKY MOURNS...

THEY SAY THAT ON THE DAY ATREUS FED HIS NEPHEWS TO THEIR FATHER THE SUN TURNED ITS FACE BACK AND HID.

AFTER THIS I EXPECT THE SUN TO TURN AWAY FOREVER. FOR ME, AT LEAST, IT'LL NEVER RISE AGAIN.

OUT!

GOOD NEWS, DAUGHTER OF TYNDAREUS...

ODYSSEUS, THE LAST GOOD NEWS *YOU* BROUGHT HAS LEFT ME NO MORE TEARS TO WEEP.

NO, LISTEN. ARTEMIS RELENTED AT THE LAST MOME-NT.

YOUR DAUGHTER WAS GLORIOUS THE WAY SHE KNELT AT THE ALTAR. THE KNIFE DESCENDED. SUDDENLY A THUNDERCLAP STUNNED US ALL. WHEN WE RECOVERED A BEAUTIFUL *DOE* LAY BEFORE THE ALTAR, PANTING OUT HER LIFEBLOOD.

A DOE...

THEN WHERE'S MY DAUGHTER?

AS WE WATCHED, A CLOUD CAME DOWN AND GATHERED HER UP. KALCHAS SAYS THE GODDESS SWEPT HER AWAY TO LIVE IN JOY WITH THE GODS.

DON'T YOU HEAR? SHE'S SAFE! YOU SHOULD BE GLAD!

GLAD? I DON'T HAVE ROOM FOR GLADNESS.

IT'S ALL CROWDED OUT BY HATE.

GO! THE WIND BLOWS SEAWARD NOW! YOUR WAY TO TROY IS OPEN!

GO ON!

I HOPE YOU ALL DIE IN THE WAR YOU'VE CREATED FOR YOURSELVES!

KLYTEMNESTRA... I CAN'T HEAR THE WORDS OF DEAD MEN.

THE RAIN'S STOPPING.

YOU'D BETTER FINISH RE-PITCHING YOUR SHIPS, NESTOR. YOU'LL NEED THEM SOON.

WELL...THAT'S DONE...

NOTHING LEFT TO STOP THE ARMY FROM SAILING.

MY PART'S PLAYED.

YOU DON'T SOUND VERY HAPPY ABOUT IT.

NEVER HAD TIME TO GO HOME TO ITHAKA.

THE HIGH KING WOULDN'T *LET* YOU GO.

HEH! HAVE YOU FORGOTTEN WHO YOU'RE TALKING TO, EURYBATES?

I COULD'VE FOUND A WAY...

BUT I DIDN'T WANT TO LEAVE THIS--THIS --WHERE I AM NOW.

WHO I AM NOW.

I'M NOT THE SAME MAN I WAS FOUR YEARS AGO IN ITHAKA. BACK THEN I PLAYED TRICKS TO *AVOID* THIS WAR.

I REMEMBER.

BUT NOW...

NOW I *WANT* TO BE HERE IN THE MIDDLE OF IT ALL, PLANNING STRATEGIES, DIRECTING THE MOVES OF MEN, TELLING THEM WHAT TO DO, HOW TO ACT, HOW TO THINK. PLAYING MY TRICKS.

I'M GOOD AT IT.

I *LIKE* IT.

BUT TONIGHT...THAT BRAVE GIRL. WHERE WOULD SHE BE NOW IF I HADN'T PLAYED MY PART? SAFE IN MYCENAE?

ODYSSEUS, YOU COULDN'T STOP WHAT THE GODS--

I COULD HAVE TRIED. IN ITHAKA I *WOULD* HAVE TRIED.

AND NIPPING AT MY HEELS COMES HALITHERSES'S PROPHECY, HOW AFTER TWENTY YEARS I'LL RETURN TO ITHAKA ALONE AND UNRECOGNIZED.

TWENTY YEARS IS A LONG TIME.

STILL...

...NOT EVEN *FORTY* YEARS COULD CHANGE MY WIFE SO MUCH THAT I WOULDN'T RECOGNIZE HER.

BUT I'M STARTING TO SEE HOW IT MIGHT HAPPEN.

HOW CAN I EXPECT ANYONE ELSE TO RECOGNIZE ME AFTER TWENTY YEARS...

...WHEN AFTER ONLY *FOUR* YEARS I FEEL AS THOUGH I WOULDN'T EVEN RECOGNIZE MYSELF?

GLOSSARY OF NAMES

Pronunciation of names can vary widely. What I present here is merely a guide and needn't be considered definitive.

Anyone seeking consistency among the forms of character and place names should look elsewhere. In general, I've used the more familiar Roman forms for the better-known characters—for instance, Achilles instead of Akhilleos, Helen instead of Helena. Lesser-known and minor characters use a more Greek form—for instance, Teukros instead of Teucer, Polydeukes instead of Pollux.

a as in lap	ee as in see	i as in sit	oo as in wool	u as in us
ay as in say	eye as in hike	o as in not	s as in less	uh as in duh
e as in bed	g as in get	oh as in note	th as in thick	

Listed alphabetically   Stress italicized syllable

Achaea a-*kee*-a, roughly the area now known as Greece
Achaeans a-*kee*-uhnz, people of Achaea, roughly modern Greece
Achilles a-*kil*-eez, son of Peleus and Thetis, prince of Phthia
Aeakus *ee*-a-kus, father of Peleus
Aegina ee-*jee*-na, Klytemnestra's servant and former nurse
Aeneas ee-*nee*-as, prince of Dardania, cousin of Trojan royal family
Agamemnon a-ga-*mem*-non, king of Mycenae, High King of the Achaeans
Aganus a-*gay*-nus, son of Paris and Helen
Agapenor a-ga-*pee*-nor, king of Arcadia
Agenor a-*jee*-nor, common ancestor of Hekuba and Helen
Aithra *ay*-thra, Helen's servant, mother of Theseus
Ajax (Great) *ay*-jax, prince of Salamis, son of Telamon
Akamas *a*-ka-mas, son of Theseus
Alkimus *al*-ki-mus, companion of Achilles
Amyntor a-*min*-tor, father of Phoenix (1)
Antenor an-*tee*-nor, Priam's councillor, Trojan elder
Antigone an-*ti*-goh-nee, cousin of Cressida
Antiphus *an*-ti-fus, from Kos, grandson of Herakles
Arcadia ar-*kay*-dee-a, area ruled by Agapenor, west of Mycenae
Argo *ar*-go, ship on quest for Golden Fleece
Argos *ar*-gos, city ruled by Diomedes
Arkas *ar*-kas, servant of Agamemnon
Arsinoe ar-*sin*-oh-ee, Iphigenia's nurse
Artemis *ar*-te-mis, goddess of the hunt and moon
Askalaphus a-*ska*-la-fus, king of Orchomenos
Asklepius as-*klee*-pee-us, greatest Achaean healer
Astyoche as-*teye*-o-kee, sister of Priam, wife of Telephus
Astyochea as-tee-o-*kee*-a, mother of Tlepolemus
Athens *a*-thenz, city in Attika, ruled by Menestheus
Atlas *at*-las, a titan
Atreus *ay*-tryoos, father of Agamemnon and Menelaus
Auge *aw*-jee, mother of Telephus
Aulis *aw*-lis, bay where army assembles
Automedon o-*to*-me-don, Achilles's charioteer
Balius *bay*-lee-us, chariot horse of Achilles
Boeotia bee-*oh*-sha, area north of Mycenae
Borus *bor*-us, father of Menesthius, brother-in-law of Achilles
Chalkiope kal-*keye*-o-pee, grandmother of Antiphus and Phiddipus
Chalkis *kal*-kis, town on the shore of Euboea opposite Aulis
Cheiron *keye*-ron, young Achilles's teacher

216

Chrysippus kreye-*sip*-us, son of Pelops, uncle of Agamemnon and Menelaus
Chrysothemis kry-*so*-the-mis, third daughter of Agamemnon and Klytemnestra
Cressida *kres*-i-duh, daughter of Kalchas
Crete *kreet,* Achaean island ruled by Idomeneus
Cyprus *seye*-prus, island recently ruled by Kinyras
Dardania dar-*day*-nee-uh, area ruled by Anchises
Dardanus *dar*-dan-us, forefather of the Trojan royal family
Deidamia dee-i-da-*meye*-uh, eldest daughter of Lykomedes of Skyros
Deiphobus de-*if*-oh-bus, prince of Troy
Delos *dee*-los, Achaean island
Demophoon dee-*mo*-foh-on, son of Theseus
Diomedes deye-o-*mee*-deez, king of Argos and Tiryns
Diores deye-*o*-reez, father of Automedon
Elektra ee-*lek*-tra, second daughter of Agamemnon and Klytemnestra
Ephyra e-fi-ra, Achaean city
Euboea yoo-*bee*-a, island ruled by Elephenor
Eudorus yoo-*dor*-us, Myrmidon
Eumenes yoo-*mee*-neez, a farmer in Lakedaemon
Eurybates yoo-*ri*-ba-teez, herald of Ithaka, companion of Odysseus
Eurypylus yoo-*ri*-pi-lus, son of Telephus and Astyoche
Guowaxeus gwo-*waks*-yoos, a farmer in Lakedaemon
Haimos *hay*-mos, Mysian warrior
Halitherses ha-li-*ther*-seez, a seer of Ithaka
Hektor *hek*-tor, eldest prince of Troy, son of Priam and Hekuba
Hekuba *he*-kyoo-ba, queen of Troy, primary wife of Priam
Helen *he*-len, wife of Menelaus, afterward wife of Paris
Helenus *he*-le-nus, Trojan prince, twin brother of Kassandra
Helikaon he-li-*kay*-on, son of Antenor
Hellespont *he*-le-spont, body of water just north of Troy
Herakles *her*-a-kleez, greatest Achaean hero
Hermione hur-*meye*-o-nee, daughter of Menelaus and Helen
Hesione he-*seye*-uh-nee, mother of Teukros, sister of Priam
Hiera heye-*eer*-uh, wife of Telephus
Ida *eye*-da, mountain near Troy
Idaeus eye-*dee*-us, Priam's herald
Idomeneus eye-do-men-yoos, king of Crete
Ilus *eye*-lus, founder of Trojan royal family, grandfather of Priam
Iphigenia i-fi-je-*neye*-a, first daughter of Agamemnon and Klytemnestra
Iphiklus *eye*-fi-klus, former king of Phylake, father of Iolaus
Ithaka *i*-tha-ka, Achaean island ruled by Odysseus
Kaikos *kay*-kos, river in Mysia
Kalchas *kal*-kas, former Trojan priest, now ally of the Achaeans
Karians *kayr*-ee-unz, area south of Troy
Kassandra ka-*san*-druh, seer daughter of Priam and Hekuba
Kastor *kas*-tor, twin of Polydeukes, brother of Helen and Klytemnestra
Katreus *kat*-ryoos, maternal grandfather of Agamemnon and Menelaus
Kebriones ke-*breye*-o-neez, son of Priam by a secondary wife
Kilissa ki-*lis*-uh, nurse of Orestes
Kinyras *kin*-i-ras, former king of Cyprus
Klymene *kli*-mee-nee, Helen's servant
Klytemnestra kleye-tem-*nes*-tra, wife of Agamemnon, sister of Helen
Kolchis *kol*-kis, city on the eastern shore of the Black Sea
Kos *kos,* Achaean island
Kreusa kree-*oo*-suh, eldest daughter of Priam and Hekuba
Kusamenos koo-sa-*mee*-nos, a farmer in Lakedaemon

217

Laerkes lay-*ur*-keez, father of Alkimus
Laertes lay-*ur*-teez, father of Odysseus
Laius *lay*-us, father of Oedipus, former king of Thebes
Lakedaemon (1) la-ke-*dee*-mon, area ruled by Menelaus
Lakedaemon (2) la-ke-*dee*-mon, grandson of Atlas, ancestor of Helen
Laodike lay-*o*-di-kee, daughter of Priam and Hekuba
Leda *lee*-da, mother of Helen
Lykia *lik*-ya, area south of Troy ruled by Sarpedon
Lykomedes leye-ko-*mee*-deez, king of Skyros, father of Deidamia
Machaon ma-*kay*-on, Achaean healer from Trikka, Podalirius's brother
Maemalus *mee*-ma-lus, father of Pisander
Melampus me-*lam*-pus, cousin of Nestor
Menelaus me-ne-*lay*-us, king of Lakedaemon, Helen's husband, Agamemnon's brother
Menestheus me-*nes*-thyoos, king of Athens
Menesthius me-*nes*-thee-us, Myrmidon son of Borus, nephew of Achilles
Menoetius men-*ee*-shus, father of Patroklus
Messenia me-*sen*-ee-a, area ruled by Nestor
Mestor *mes*-tor, prince of Troy
Mnemon *nee*-mon, guide assigned to Achilles by Thetis
Mycenae meye-*see*-nee, Achaean city ruled by Agamemnon
Mycenaean meye-see-*nee*-an, of the area ruled by Agamemnon
Myrmidons *mur*-mi-donz, Achilles's soldiers
Mysia *mi*-sha, area south of Troy where Telephus rules
Mysians *mi*-shanz, people of the area south of Troy where Telephus rules
Nauplia *naw*-plee-uh, area ruled by Nauplius on coast of Argolid
Nauplius *naw*-plee-us, father of Palamedes and Oeax, king of Nauplia
Neleus *neel*-yoos, father of Nestor
Neoptolemus nee-op-*to*-le-mus, son of Achilles and Deidamia
Nereid *nee*-ree-id, title of Thetis, the daughter of Nereus
Nestor *nes*-tor, elderly king of Pylos
Odysseus o-*dis*-yoos, king of Ithaka
Oedipus *ed*-i-pus or *ee*-di-pus, king of Thebes, grandfather/uncle of Thersander
Opois *o*-poh-is, Achaean city
Orchomenos or-*ko*-me-nus, city ruled by Askalaphus
Orestes oh-*res*-teez, son of Agamemnon and Klytemnestra
Paeonians pee-*oh*-nee-unz, area northwest of Troy, beyond Thrace
Palamedes pa-la-*mee*-deez, prince of Nauplia
Pandarus *pan*-da-rus, uncle of Cressida, brother of Kalchas
Panthous *pan*-thoh-us, Trojan elder
Paris *pa*-ris, Trojan prince, lover of Helen
Patara pa-*tar*-a, city in Lykia
Patroklus pa-*trok*-lus, Achilles's closest companion
Peirithous peye-*rith*-oh-us, Achaean hero, brother of Phisadie, father of Polypoetes
Peleus *peel*-yoos, father of Achilles, king of Phthia
Pelops *pel*-ops, paternal grandfather of Agamemnon and Menelaus
Peneleos pee-*ne*-lee-os, Boeotian commander
Penelope pe-*nel*-o-pee, wife of Odysseus
Periboea pe-ri-*bee*-uh, mother of Great Ajax
Phalis *fay*-lis, king of Sidon
Phidippus feye-*dip*-us, from Kos, grandson of Herakles
Philoktetes fi-lok-*tee*-teez, king of Methone
Phoenicia fee-*ni*-sha, area on the coast of the Levant
Phoenix (1) *fee*-niks, companion of Achilles
Phoenix (2) *fee*-niks, son of Agenor

Phrygia *fri*-ja, area northeast of Troy
Phthia *ftheye*-a, area of Achaea ruled by Peleus
Pisander peye-*san*-der, a Myrmidon
Pleione pleye-*oh*-nee, lover of Atlas, ancestor of both Helen and the Trojan royal line
Pleisthenes plee-*is*-the-neez, son of Helen and Menelaus
Podalirius po-da-*leye*-ree-us, Achaean healer from Trikka, brother of Machaon
Podarge po-*dar*-jee, mare given to Peleus by the gods
Poliwos po-*lee*-wos, a farmer in Lakedaemon
Polydamas po-*li*-da-mas, son of Panthous, companion of Hektor
Polydeukes po-li-*dyoo*-keez, twin of Kastor, brother of Helen and Klytemnestra
Polydora po-li-*dor*-a, sister of Achilles
Polyneikes po-li-*neye*-keez, son of Oedipus, father of Thersander
Polypoetes po-li-*pee*-teez, son of Peirithous, nephew of Phisadie
Poseidon poh-*seye*-don, god of the sea and earthquake
Priam *preye*-am, king of Troy
Pylos *peye*-los, area ruled by Nestor
Pyrrha *peer*-uh, Achilles's name in female disguise
Pyrrhus *peer*-us, original name of son of Achilles and Deidamia
Rhodes *rohdz,* Achaean island ruled by Tlepolemus
Salamis *sa*-la-mis, Achaean island ruled by Telamon
Sarpedon sar-*pee*-don, king of Lykia
Sidon *seye*-don, area on the coast of the Levant
Skaean Gate *skee*-an, a gate of Troy
Skyros *skeye*-ros, island ruled by Lykomedes
Skythia *ski*-thee-a, area northeast of Troy across the Black Sea
Sparta *spar*-tuh, city ruled by Menelaus
Spercheus spur-*kee*-us, river in Phthia
Sthenelus *sthen*-e-lus, companion of Diomedes
Talthybius tal-*thi*-bee-us, Agamemnon's herald
Tantalus *tan*-ta-lus, great-grandfather of Agamemnon and Menelaus
Tegea te-*jee*-a, Achaean city
Telamon *tel*-a-mon, king of Salamis, father of Ajax and Teukros
Telemachus te-*lem*-a-kus, son of Odysseus and Penelope
Telephus *te*-le-fus, king of Mysia, son of Herakles
Teukros *tyoo*-kros, half-brother of Ajax, son of Telamon and Hesione
Teuthrania tyooth-*ran*-ya, Mysian city
Teuthranius tyooth-*ran*-yus, half-brother of Telephus
Teuthras *tyooth*-ras, former king of Teuthrania
Thebans *thee*-banz, people of Thebes
Thebes *theebz,* Achaean city ruled by Thersander
Thersander ther-*san*-der, king of Thebes
Thersites ther-*seye*-teez, cousin of Diomedes
Theseus *thees*-yoos, Achaean hero, former king of Athens
Thessalus *thes*-a-lus, father of Antiphus and Phidippus
Thetis *thee*-tis, Achaean priestess, mother of Achilles
Thrace *thrays,* area northwest of Troy across the Hellespont
Thyestes theye-*es*-teez, brother of Atreus, uncle of Agamemnon and Menelaus
Thymoetes theye-*mee*-teez, Trojan elder
Tlepolemus tle-*po*-le-mus, king of Rhodes, son of Herakles
Trikka *trik*-a, Achaean city of Podalirius and Machaon
Troilus *troy*-lus, prince of Troy
Tyndareus tyn-*dar*-yoos, father of Helen and Klytemnestra
Xanthus *zan*-thus, chariot horse of Achilles
Zeus *zyoos,* greatest of the gods

219

GENEALOGICAL CHART: THE ACHAEANS

Characters in bold appear and are named in *Sacrifice*.

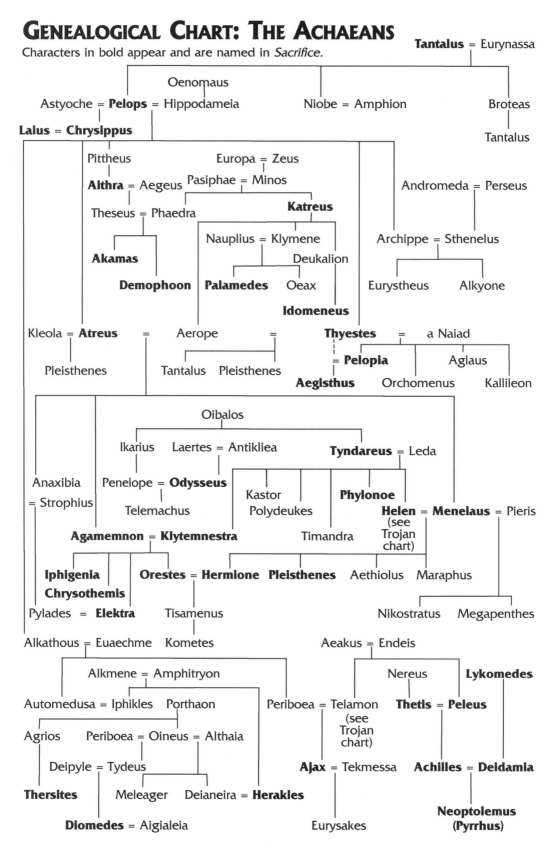

GENEALOGICAL CHART: THE TROJAN ROYAL FAMILY

Characters in bold appear and are named in *Sacrifice*.

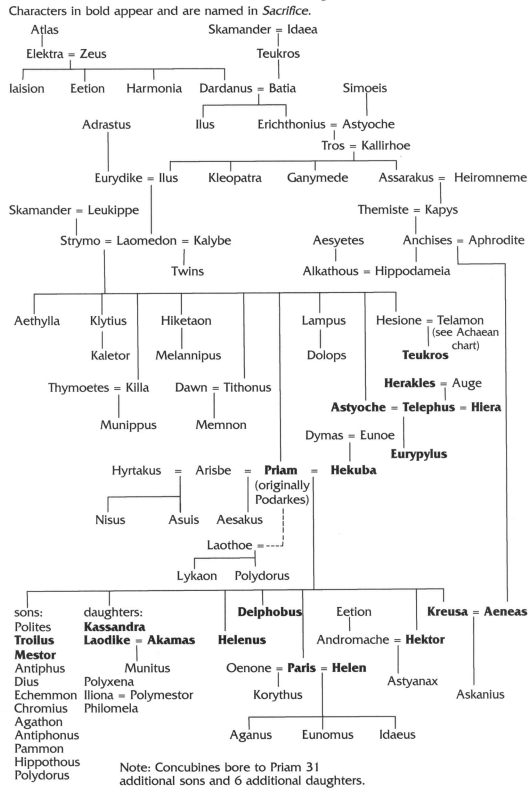

BIBLIOGRAPHY

The following list of sources is an addendum to the list in the previous volume, *A Thousand Ships.*

THE STORY

Aeschylus. *Agamemnon. Libation Bearers. Eumenides. Fragments.* Trans. Herbert Weir Smith (Loeb Classical Library). Cambridge and London: Harvard University Press, 1999. (Orig. edition 1926.)

Alkaios. "Helen and Thetis." In *Greek Lyric Poetry.* Trans. Willis Barnstone. New York: Bantam Books, 1962.

Atwood, E. Bagby and Virgil K. Whitaker, eds. *Excidium Troiae.* Cambridge: The Medieval Academy of America, 1944.

Bacchylides. *Complete Poems.* Trans. Robert Fagles, new edition. New Haven, CT and London: Yale University Press, 1998.

Brewer's Dictionary of Phrase and Fable, revised and enlarged. New York: Harper & Brothers Publishers, n.d.

Burgess, Jonathan S. *The Tradition of the Trojan War in Homer and the Epic Cycle.* Baltimore and London: The Johns Hopkins University Press, 2001.

Bush, Douglas. *Mythology and the Renaissance Tradition in English Poetry.* New York: Pageant Book Company, 1957.

de Pizan, Christine. *The Book of the City of Ladies.* Trans. Rosalind Brown-Grant. London: Penguin Books, 1999.

Euripides. *Electra.* Produced and directed by Michael Cacoyannis. 1 hour 53 minutes. Metro Goldwyn Mayer, 1962. Digital virtual disc.

Feder, Theodore H. "Iphigenia and Isaac, Saved at the Altar." *Archaeology Odyssey* 5 (May/June 2002): 50-62.

Forsdyke, John. *Greece Before Homer, Ancient Chronology and Mythology.* London: Max Parrish, 1956.

Gibbs, A.C. *The Gest Hystoriale of the Destruction of Troy.* In *Middle English Romances.* Evanston, IL: Northwestern University Press, 1966.

Gluck, Christoph Willibald. *Iphigenie en Aulide.* Libretto by Marie Francois Louis Gand Bailli du Roullet dit Le Blanc. Trans. John Sidgwick. Monteverdi Choir. Orchestre de L'opera de Lyon. Conducted by John Eliot Gardiner. N.P.: Radio France - Erato Disques, 1990.

Greek Epic Fragments from the Seventh to the Fifth Centuries BC. Trans. Martin L. West (Loeb Classical Library). Cambridge and London: Harvard University Press, 2003.

Haggard, H. Rider and Andrew Lang. *The World's Desire.* New York: A Del Rey Book published by Ballantine Books, 1972.

Henryson, Robert. *Testament of Cresseid,* ed. Denton Fox. London: Thomas Nelson and Sons Ltd., 1968.

Hutchinson, W.M.L. *The Sunset of the Heroes.* London: J.M. Dent & Co. and New York: E.P. Dutton & Co., 1911.

Huxley, G.L. *Greek Epic Poetry from Eumelos to Panyasis.* Cambridge: Harvard University Press, 1969.

Joseph of Exeter. *Trojan War I-III.* Trans. A.K. Bate. Warminster, Wiltshire: Bolchazy - Carducci Publishers/Aris & Phillips Ltd., 1986.

Landor, Walter Savage. "The Abbe Delille and Walter Landor." In *The Works of Walter Savage Landor,* vol. I. London: Chapman and Hall, 1868.

Landor, Walter Savage. *Pericles and Aspasia,* "Laodamia" and "Menelaus and Helen." In *The Works of Walter Savage Landor,* vol. II. London: Chapman and Hall, 1868.

Lydgate, John. *Troy Book: Selections,* ed. Robert R. Edwards. Kalamazoo, MI: Medieval Institute Publications for Western Michigan University, 1998.

Morris, William. "The Death of Paris." In *The Earthly Paradise, a Poem,* part III. Boston: Roberts Brothers, 1870.

Mozart, Wolfgang Amadeus. *Idomeneo: King of Crete.* Libretto by Giovanni Battista Varesco. Directed by Lofti Mansouri. San Diego Opera, April 2001.

Norris III, Frank Pelletier. *La Coronica Troyana: A Medieval Spanish Translation of Guido de Colonna's Historia Destructionis Troiae.* University of North Carolina's Studies in the Romance Languages and Literatures, No. 90. Chapel Hill, NC: University of North Carolina Press, 1970.

O'Neill, Eugene. *Mourning Becomes Electra.* UCSD Theatre & Dance, San Diego, CA, November 2002.

Peele, George. "Tale of Troy" and "Araygnement of Paris." In *The Life and Works of George Peele,* vol. 3. New Haven and London: Yale University Press, 1970.

Philostratus, Flavius. *Heroikos.* Trans. Jennifer K. Berenson Maclean and Ellen Bradshaw Aitken. Atlanta, GA: Society of Biblical Literature, 2001.

Pindar. *The Odes of Pindar.* Trans. Sir John Sandys (Loeb Classical Library). Cambridge: Harvard University Press, 1957.

Plautus. *The Two Bacchides.* In *The Complete Roman Drama,* vol. 1, ed. George E. Duckworth. Trans. Edward H. Sugden. New York: Random House, 1942.

Rossetti, Dante Gabriel. "Troy Town." In *Victorian Poetry and Poetics,* 2nd edition, ed. Houghton and Stange. Boston: Houghton Mifflin Company, 1968.

Sappho. "To Anaktoria, Now a Soldier's Wife in Lydia" and "Wedding of Andromache." In *Greek Lyric Poetry.* Trans. Willis Barnstone. New York: Bantam Books, 1962.

Sophocles. *Fragments.* Trans. Hugh Lloyd-Jones (Loeb Classical Library). Cambridge and London: Harvard University Press, 1996.

The Trojan War in Greek Art, A Picture Book. Boston: Museum of Fine Arts, [1975].

The Trojan Women. Produced by Michael Cacoyannis and Anis Nohra. 105 minutes. Family Home Entertainment, Inc., 1971. Videocassette.

Wordsworth, William. "When Philoctetes in the Lemnian Isle" and "Laodamia." In *The Shorter Poems of William Wordsworth.* London: J.M. Dent & Co. and New York: E.P. Dutton & Co., 1907.

Young, Arthur M. *Troy and Her Legend.* Pittsburgh, PA: University of Pittsburgh Press, 1948.

THE SETTINGS IN GENERAL

Carpenter, Rhys. *Discontinuity in Greek Civilization.* New York: The Norton Library, W.W. Norton & Company, Inc., 1968.

Connolly, Peter. *The Ancient Greece of Odysseus.* Oxford: Oxford University Press, 1998.

Leaf, Walter. *Troy, a Study in Homeric Geography.* London: Macmillan and Co., Limited, 1912.

Miller, Olive Beaupre and Harry Neal Baum. *My Book of History, A Picturesque Tale of Progress,* vol. 2, Conquests. Chicago and Toronto: The Bookhouse for Children, 1930.

Page, Denys L. *History and the Homeric Iliad.* Berkeley, CA and Los Angeles: University of California Press, 1963.

Sandars, N.K. *The Sea Peoples: Warriors of the Ancient Mediterranean, 1250-1150 BC.* London: Thames & Hudson, 1978.

TROY

Easton D.F., J.D. Hawkins, A.G. Sherratt, and E.S. Sherratt. "Troy in Recent Perspective." *Anatolian Studies* 52 (2002): 75-109.

Studia Troica. Band 9. Mainz am Rhein: Verlag Phillip von Zabern, 1999.

Studia Troica. Band 10. Mainz am Rhein: Verlag Phillip von Zabern, 2000.

Studia Troica. Band 11. Mainz am Rhein: Verlag Phillip von Zabern, 2001.

THE CHARACTERS

King, Katherine Callen. *Achilles, Paradigms of the War Hero from Homer to the Middle Ages.* Berkeley, CA: University of California Press, 1987.

Kleinbaum, Abby Wettan. *The War Against the Amazons.* New York: New Press, McGraw-Hill Book Company, 1983.

Mackie, Hilary. *Talking Trojan, Speech and Community in the Iliad.* Lanham, Boulder, New York, and London: Rowman & Littlefield Publishers, Inc., n.d.

Michelakis, Pantelis. *Achilles in Greek Tragedy.* Cambridge: Cambridge University Press, n.d.

Percy III, William Armstrong. *Pederasty and Pedagogy in Archaic Greece.* Urbana, IL and Chicago: University of Illinois Press, 1996.

Wilde, Lyn Webster. *On the Trail of the Women Warriors, the Amazons in Myth and History.* New York: Thomas Dunne Books, St. Martin's Press, 2000.

THE MYCENAEANS

Desbrough, V.R. *The Last Mycenaeans and Their Successors.* Oxford: Clarendon Press, 1964.

French, Elizabeth. *Mycenae, Agamemnon's Capital.* Stroud, Goucestershire and Charleston, SC: Tempus, 2002.

Levin, Saul. *The Linear B Decipherment Controversy Re-examined.* New York: State University of New York, 1964.

Palmer, L.R. *The Interpretations of Mycenaean Greek Texts.* London: Oxford University Press, 1963.

Tarsouli, Georgia. *Mystras—Sparta.* Athens: M. Pechlivanides and Co. S.A., n.d.

Ventris, Michael and John Chadwick. *Documents in Mycenaean Greek.* London: Cambridge University Press, 1956.

image® COMICS

BACKLIST

MORE GREAT TITLES FROM IMAGE

A DISTANT SOIL VOL I
THE GATHERING
ISBN: 1-887259-51-2
STAR07382

AGE OF BRONZE VOL I
A THOUSAND SHIPS
ISBN: 1-58240-200-0
STAR13458

AVIGON
ISBN: 1-58240-182-9
STAR11946

BLACK FOREST
ISBN: 1-58240-350-3
JAN041286

BLUNTMAN AND CHRONIC
ISBN: 1-58240-208-6
STAR13070

BULLETPROOF MONK
ISBN: 1-58240-244-2
STAR16331

BUNKER, THE
ISBN: 1-58240-296-5
STAR18864

CHASING DOGMA
ISBN: 1-58240-206-X
STAR13071

CLERKS
THE COMIC BOOKS
ISBN: 1-58240-209-4
STAR13071

DIORAMAS, A LOVE STORY
ISBN: 1-58240-359-7
FEB041312

DAWN VOL II
RETURN OF THE GODDESS
ISBN: 1-58240-242-6
STAR15771

DELICATE CREATURES
ISBN: 1-58240-225-6
STAR14906

GOLDFISH
THE DEFINITIVE COLLECTION
ISBN: 1-58240-195-0
STAR13576

GRRL SCOUTS, VOL.1
ISBN: 1-58240-316-3
STAR19476

GRRL SCOUTS, VOL. 2:
WORK SUCKS
ISBN: 1-58240-343-0
DEC031320

HEAVEN LLC.
ISBN: 1-58240-351-1
JAN041297

JINX
THE DEFINITIVE COLLECTION
ISBN: 1-58240-179-9
STAR13039

KABUKI, VOL I
CIRCLE OF BLOOD
ISBN: 1-88727-9-806
STAR12480

KANE, VOL. 1:
WELCOME TO NEW EDEN
ISBN: 1-58240-340-6
NOV031264

LAZARUS CHURCHYARD
THE FINAL CUT
ISBN: 1-58240-180-2
STAR12720

LEAVE IT TO CHANCE, VOL I:
SHAMAN'S RAIN
ISBN: 1-58240-253-1
STAR16641

LIBERTY MEADOWS, VOL I:
EDEN
ISBN: 1-58240-260-4
STAR16143

MAGE
THE HERO DEFINED, VOL I
ISBN: 1-58240-012-1
STAR08160

NOWHERESVILLE
ISBN: 1-58240-241-8
STAR15904

PARLIAMENT OF JUSTICE
ISBN: 1-58240-
STAR19476

POWERS, VOL I:
WHO KILLED RETRO GIRL?
ISBN: 1-58240-223-X
STAR12482

PvP: THE DORK AGES
ISBN: 1-58240-345-7
DEC031330

SHANGRI-LA
ISBN: 1-58240-352-X
NOV031270

TORSO
THE DEFINITIVE COLLECTION
ISBN: 1-58240-174-8
STAR12688

WHISKEY DICKEL
INTERNATIONAL COWGIRL
ISBN: 1-58240-318-X
STAR19501

ZORRO
THE COMPLETE ALEX TOTH
ISBN: 1-58240-090-3
STAR14527

IMAGECOMICS.COM
DIRECT SALES

001 11

7 09853 00148 5

For The Comic
Shop Near You
Carrying Comics
And Collections
From Image
Comics, Please
Call Toll Free
1-888-Comic Book.